John Hume

A Sermon preached before the Incorporated Society for the

Propagation of the Gospel in Foreign Parts

John Hume

A Sermon preached before the Incorporated Society for the Propagation of the Gospel in Foreign Parts

ISBN/EAN: 9783741197192

Manufactured in Europe, USA, Canada, Australia, Japa

Cover: Foto ©Thomas Meinert / pixelio.de

Manufactured and distributed by brebook publishing software (www.brebook.com)

John Hume

A Sermon preached before the Incorporated Society for the Propagation of the Gospel in Foreign Parts

A

SERMON

Preached before the

Incorporated S O C I E T Y

FOR THE

Propagation of the Gospel in Foreign Parts ;

AT THEIR

ANNIVERSARY MEETING

IN THE

Parish Church of St. Mary-le-Bow,

On FRIDAY *February* 19, 1762.

By the Right Reverend Father in GOD,
JOHN Lord Bishop of *OXFORD*.

L O N D O N :

Printed by E. OWEN and T. HARRISON in
Warwick-Lane ; and Sold by A. MILLAR
at *Buchanan*'s Head in the *Strand*.

MDCCLXII.

*At the Anniverſary Meeting of the Society
for the* Propagation of the Goſpel in
Forcign Parts, *in the* Veſtry Room *of*
St. Mary-le-Bow, *on* Friday *the* 19th
Day of February, 1762.

A G R E E D, that the Thanks of
the S o c i e t y be given to the
Right Reverend the Lord Biſhop of
Oxford, for his Sermon preached this
Day before the S o c i e t y ; and that
his Lordſhip be defired to deliver a
Copy of the fame to the S o c i e t y
to be Printed.

Daniel Burton, Secretary.

St. MAT. Ch. ix. Ver. 36, 37, 38.

When he faw the multitudes, he was moved with compaffion on them, becaufe they fainted, and were fcattered abroad, as fheep having no fhepherd. Then faith he unto his difciples—The harveft truly is plenteous, but the labourers are few. Pray ye therefore the Lord of the harveft, that he will fend forth labourers into his harveft.

WE read in the words preceding my text, that Jefus went about all the cities and villages, teaching in their fynagogues, and preaching the gofpel of the kingdom. And as he paffed through the Fields, the people flocked after him, in great numbers, to hear his doctrines, and fee

the

the mighty works which he did. It was probably fummer, and about the time of harveft—the fheep fainting with heat upon the mountains, and the valleys already white with corn. To thefe he alludes in the words of my text, where it follows, that, *when he faw the multitudes, he had compaffion on them, becaufe they appeared to him, as fheep having no fhepherd* to lead them to their refrefhment ; and as the ears of corn, juft ripe for the fickle, but in danger of perifhing where they ftood, for want of labourers to gather, and lay them up in the garner ; that is, for want of teachers to prepare, and fit them for a place in that kingdom which he preached. *Then faith he unto his difciples, the harveft truly is plenteous, but the labourers are few : pray ye therefore the Lord of the harveft, that he will fend forth labourers into his harveft.*

The words, fo explained, will lead us to examine—Firft,

The grounds and reafons of our Saviour's compaffion ;

Secondly—His inftruction to his difciples in confequence of his compaffion—*Pray ye therefore the Lord of the harveft, that he will fend forth labourers into his harveft.*

The

To begin with the firft—namely,

The grounds and reafons of our Saviour's compaffion for the multitudes.

They are here defcribed as fheep, not having a fhepherd, fcattered, and fainting for want of refrefhment; and yet, it is evident in this place, that it was not the want of bodily refrefhment, that moved his compaffion—no—it was a want of a very different kind—a want of knowledge, inftruction, and direction—the knowledge of thofe faving truths which he came to reveal—inftruction in the ways of falvation, from which they had wandered—and direction, where to find that reft for their fouls, which could be found only through himfelf.

Thefe were wants, of which they themfelves were not confcious; and yet they were fuch, as, in the eyes of our merciful Redeemer, appeared more deplorable, than the want of their daily food. He faw them fainting under the burden of their fins, and in danger of perifhing in them, for want of that bread of life, which he alone could give; that pardon for their fins, which he alone could purchafe for them.

The real ftate of the multitudes feems probably to be this—a fet of thoughtlefs, illiterate, untutoured, creatures; fubject by their low fta-

tion

tion to the guidance of thofe, who had *fhut up
the key of knowledge* from them, and yet, by their
behaviour appearing humble, and teachable, and
difpofed to hear the gofpel of the kingdom of
Heaven.

But here it may be asked—How does it appear, that their cafe was pitiable? that they
were either out of the way, and had not proper
guides—or, that they wanted any knowledge,
that was neceffary to faivation. They had a law
written in their confciences, the law of nature,
to follow—they had alfo a revealed law—the
law of Mofes, and the Prophets. Could they
not follow thefe? or, was not their inftruction
fufficient?

To thefe queftions it might be anfwered
in general—that—notwithftanding their having
both a law of nature, and a revealed law, yet,
if they had tranfgreffed or mifunderftood both
thefe laws, they certainly wanted, both inftruction, and reformation, and were therefore fit ob-
jects of our Saviour's compaffion. Had they
rightly underftood the law, and the Prophets,
thofe would have led them to ask inftruction of
him, in whom both the law and the Prophets
were fulfilled. I might further add, that—had
they underftood, and obeyed the great principles
of morality, as founded in reafon and nature,
                                                    thofe

thofe alfo would have led them to embrace the doctrines of Chrift.

But I fhall confider, more particularly, this pretended fufficiency of the law of nature.

By the law of nature, may be underftood—either—all thofe truths that are difcoverable in the nature of things, by the natural faculties of man—or elfe—fuch notices only of truth, as each man's particular faculties enable him to acquire.

In the firft fenfe of the law of nature, the multitude certainly could have no fuch law, nor indeed can any one ; for who is there will fay, he poffeffes all that knowledge of the nature of things which is poffible to be attained by man ?

In the fecond fenfe of a law of nature, the multitude certainly had it—but, in proportion to their refpective defects of underftanding, this law of nature was defective ; it could not, of itfelf, direct them to all that happinefs, and perfection, of which their nature was capable. If therefore our Saviour had certain doctrines to reveal to them, conducive to their happinefs, but not difcoverable by their own natural faculties, there was evidently a want of fo divine an inftructor, to fupply thofe defects, and difcover to them the way to their true happinefs. We

muſt enquire therefore what thoſe truths or doctrines were, and in what ſenſe it was eſſential to
their happineſs to be inſtructed in them.

Now of theſe, it will be ſufficient, to our preſent purpoſe, to mention only the following—
namely—*That God ſo loved the world, that he ſent
his Son into the world, that all men through him
might be ſaved,* that this Son of God ſhould teach
the will of his heavenly Father, that he ſhould
die for the ſins of mankind, ſhould riſe again
for their juſtification, ſhould ſend his Holy Spirit
into their hearts to ſanctify them, ſhould raiſe
them up from death, and, *at the end of the world,
ſhould come again with power, and great glory, to
judge the world in righteouſneſs, and render to every
man according to his works.*

Theſe were ſome of the divine doctrines which
he came to teach ; and, that the truth of theſe
could never have been diſcovered, by the bulk
of mankind, through the uſe of their natural faculties, is needleſs to prove, becauſe abſurd to
ſuppoſe.

The only remaining queſtion is, Wherein
conſiſted the advantage of being inſtructed in
them ? What need of more light, than what our
common nature gives us ?

In anſwer to this, I cannot help previouſly ob-
ſerving ; that this is a queſtion, which cannot
wiſely

wifely be asked, either by a Chriftian, or an Infidel. A Chriftian cannot ask it confiftently with
his faith ; becaufe, to fuppofe there is no need of
any further light, than what our common nature
gives, fuppofes the Gofpel ufelefs, and contradicts
the end of Chrift's coming into the world.
Neither can an Infidel, confiftently with his un-
belief of a future ftate, afk, with more pro-
priety, — *What need of more light, than what
our common nature gives?* for unlefs our common nature has enabled every one to difcern,
and attain all that happinefs, which he is formed
capable of enjoying; there muft neceffarily be
a want of happinefs, arifing from this want of
difcernment; and furely—when we are daily
plunging into evils, for want of light to forefee
and efcape them— when we are daily lofing the
benefit of life itfelf, that is, on this fuppofition,
the benefit of our whole exiftence, for want of
knowledge to efcape the danger— it is very abfurd to afk gravely—what need have we of more
light ?

 But to proceed—The queftion— *What need of
more light, than what our common nature gives?*
—implies a conceffion, that fome light is needful. Now if any degree of light is acknowledged
needful, it muft be needful for the attainment of

B   fome

some end, some good to the being to whom it is needful. Unless therefore every the greatest possible good, is equally discoverable by any the least possible degree of light, as it is by the greatest, a greater light must always be needful, for the attainment of such ends, as lie beyond the reach of a lesser light.

But to come more directly to the point. The question—*what need of more light?* plainly implies, that *more* light would be useless.

Now to determine precisely—how much light, and no more, is useful, or sufficient, for the direction of moral agents, is rather difficult. The intellects of mankind are so unequal, there can be no common standard fixed, which can be a rule to all. If you take the measure of a sufficient rule, from the strongest, and most improved understandings, you absolutely exclude the bulk of mankind from having any rule at all.—If you take it from the lowest degree of intellect, that is to be found in the species, you make every higher degree of intellect useless, and superfluous. Now, as it cannot be supposed, either that our Creator has given superior faculties, and powers to one part of the species, for no useful purpose—or left the other part without any rule

rule at all, we may reasonably infer—First, That every accountable being has a rule of action proportioned to his natural power of using it. But secondly,· That as the faculties and powers of each are different, and capable of being improved in different degrees, there must necessarily be a difference also in the rule given to each. The rule must be·adapted, and made level to the powers of the agent that is to be ruled by it. Thirdly therefore, from the·different powers given, and the different rules adapted to the respective powers of each, we must infer a difference also in the ends, for the attainment of which these powers, and these rules are given, otherwise it must be maintained, that the greatest powers which God can give, can carry us to no higher end than the least, consequently, that it is a matter of absolute indifference, whether we are placed in the highest, or lowest. rank of intelligent accountable creatures. Lastly,

As happiness, or good, is the only end for which any powers, any rule, or directing light, can be wanted, or desired by an intelligent being, the value of every rule must be rated, both by the rectitude of its direction, and the importance of the end, for which its direction is wanted. The man, who has a rule to direct him only to

a lefs good, has certainly not fo valuable a rule,
as he who has a rule to direct him to a greater
good. Confequently — The man, whofe intellects are too low to difcover, or too pre-
poffeffed with error to admit the guidance of
a higher rule, cannot poffibly, through the
direction of this inferior rule, arrive at the fame
end, to which a higher rule could have carried
him.

For Inftance—There is a twylight of underftanding, which has only fome faint, imperfect
notices of right, and wrong; and thefe, per-
haps, obfcured by paffion, and prejudice. Let
us fuppofe it the cafe of a wild Indian, ignorant
of the True God, and ignorant of any reafon,
or fitnefs of things, but what agrees with the
natural dictates of his own heart, or the man-
ners and cuftoms of thofe among whom he
lives. Be thefe ever fo barbarous, or abfurd,
they are to him the ftandard of right and
wrong, the point of honour and ambition. He
follows them, not only without remorfe, or felf-
reproach, but with felf-approbation. Thus he
invents the keeneft torments for his enemy, in-
flicts them with all the coolnefs of deliberate
reafon, and exults in the anguifh he can make
him fuffer. —Will any one fay —what need is
there

there to humanize this Barbarian? Will any one
fay—Why is not his brutal nature as good as the
moft amiable of the human fpecies? Why is
not the doctrine which teaches him to inflict
the moft exquifite torments on his enemies, as
beneficial a doctrine, and as good a rule, as
that of our Saviour, *Love your enemies, do good
to them that hate you?* —You cannot fay it, if
your heart can feel for others; you would not
fay it, was you to feel the torments inflicted on
yourfelf.

But, examine the contrary character——

Suppofe, for Inftance, a mind filled with all
the knowledge, and all the virtues, that Chrift
has taught us; all the gratitude to God, which
a fenfe of infinite obligation can infpire; and all
the inward joy, which the certain hope of everlafting happinefs can beftow.—I beg leave then
to afk—Is there any difference of advantage between thefe characters? and, if there is, to what
is it owing? Is it not to the different light im-
parted to each, which gives the different rule
of action? Will any one venture to affirm, that
the morality, the virtue, the happinefs of the
one, is equal to that of the other? or, that 't
appears to be the intention of their comm t
Creator, that they fhould be equaly happy

confequel. .

confequence of their refpective rules and actions. For in fact it cannot be : it is contrary to the eftablifhed laws of nature, that it fhould be fo. Nature never gives equal happinefs, where it gives not equal powers and capacities proper to receive it.

Upon the whole then—If our Saviour taught the multitude a more perfect rule of action, than what they had before : If he placed before them their true happinefs, and moft valuable end, in a more confpicuous light ; and gave them ftronger reafons, and motives to purfue it, it is abfurd to afk—what advantage had they from it ? They had the advantage of a more important end fet before them, and the Guidance of a more direct rule to attain it.

In confequence of this—They had the advantage of new powers given ; a new fphere of action opened, for the exercife, the improvement, and extent of their virtues : they had new joys fpringing up in their fouls, from ideas, before inconceivable by them, of the mercy, and goodnefs of God to mankind through Jefus Chrift. — The rule of action, whofe end, as pointed out by the feeble light of nature, was in general, to pafs innocently, and quietly through a fhort, precarious duration here, to an

uncertain,

uncertain, unaffured hereafter—this rule, I fay, was immediately directed to a higher end, the attainment of happinefs eternal in the Heavens, through the brighter light of the Gofpel. To doubt whether thefe were advantages, is, in other words, to doubt, whether the knowledge of our Creator's goodnefs is better than ignorance; whether truth is a better rule than falfehood; whether light is a better guide than darknefs; whether a fure and certain hope of a bleffed immortality, through faith in Chrift, be more conducive to happinefs, than fear, doubt, and perplexity.

Having thus endeavoured to explain the grounds, and reafons of our Saviour's compaffion for the multitudes; I proceed, in the fecond place, to confider—

The inftruction given to his difciples, in confequence of his compaffion — *Pray ye therefore the Lord of the harveft, that he will fend forth labourers into his harveft.*

This command of our Saviour's, though directed more immediately to his difciples, who then attended him, yet, every good Chriftian will confider it as directed to himfelf. He will make it his prayer to God, that he would fend forth teachers, to difpenfe the bleffings of his word;

word ; and will join his endeavours to his prayers, that the bleffing may be diffufed as wide as
poffible. The fame benevolent fpirit, which
moved our Saviour to compaffionate the wants
of our common nature, ought certainly to be in
us, who call ourfelves his difciples, and move
us to the fame compaffion one for another.—
But it is needlefs, before this audience, to enforce the duty. We are here affembled to teftify
the fenfe we have of the common obligation—
to unite our beft endeavours—and to implore the
bleffing of God on the labours of this Society,
for the fupport, and propagation of his Gofpel.

The peculiar circumftances of the prefent
time are fuch, that we ourfelves can make the
fame reflection now, which our Saviour made,
in the words of my text, on feeing the multitudes—*The harveft truly is plenteous, but the labourers are few.* A new. field is now open to
our labour. By the bleffing of God on his Ma-
jefty's arms, it ftretches itfelf to the utmoft parts
of the globe. Our armies have gone before us ;
they have made the moft diftant countries ac-
ceffible to our miffionaries, and brought multitudes innumerable within the reach of our inftruction. But where, in this *wildernefs,* can
be found *bread from Heaven* fufficient to fatisfy.
their

their wants? Their wild, untutor'd minds remain in the fame favage ftate of ignorance, in
which they were found. Their fuperftition,
their prejudices, their brutal habits and inclina-
tions remain ftill unconquered. Our fword carried no inftruction with it : It made them own,
and obey a fuperior on earth ; but it could not
force their intellects; it could not open their hearts
to receive, and obey a higher Mafter in Heaven,
the one *true God, and Jefus Chrift whom he has fent.*

This victory over their hearts can be gained
only by the force of truth, by the word of God.
But truth has no force, where it is not perceiv-
ed; nor the word of God, where it is not pub-
lifhed. Teachers therefore muft be fent to explain, and enforce it ; and thefe in fome proportion to the numbers that want it : New
fchools of virtue muft be founded—new femi-
naries of religion planted—new Churches for
divine worfhip erected—All thefe cares, for the
further propagation of the Gofpel, come now
under the attention of this Society ; befides what
cometh upon them daily, the care of all the
churches already planted, and the prefervation
of our holy faith, already taught, and eftablifhed.
But what Society of men is, of itfelf, fufficient
for this? The plenteoufnefs of the harveft, ex-

C   ceeds

ceeds the powers of our labour to gather it.—
We muft pray the *Lord of the harveft, that he
will fend forth labourers*—The fame good Providence, which, beyond all human expectation,
has opened this extent of country to our victo-
rious forces, can equaly open it for the entrance
of his word, and may, for that very reafon,
have already opened it to our arms, in order to
make a way for his truth to follow them. *The
Sowers*, therefore, *muft go forth to fow the feed*;
and however fmall its fuccefs may at firft appear,
we have no reafon to defpair of its future
growth. We know to what our Saviour has
likened the kingdom of Heaven ; and we have
feen it verified in the fuccefs of our paft labours. *The kingdom of Heaven is like unto a
grain of muftard-feed ; which a man took, and
fowed in his field : which indeed is the leaft of all
feeds ; but, when it is grown, it is the greateft
among herbs, and becometh a tree ; fo that the
birds of the air come, and lodge in the branches
thereof.*

  The end, and defign of this Society is, not
only to maintain, and preferve in its purity, the
religion of Chrift, as already preached in thofe
Parts, but, at the fame time, to extend the be-
nefits of its doctrines, if poffible, to all mankind.

kind. This is the end, to which all our labours are, and ought to be, directed. And a
moft worthy end it is — the moft excellent, that
a reafonable, and good being can purfue. It
is — to lead men, by the help of faith in God's
word, through the practice of every virtue, to
all that peace, which can be enjoyed on earth,
and to a fitnefs, through the mediation of Chrift,
to receive everlafting happinefs in Heaven—It
is, through the affiftance of God's grace, revealed
in his gofpel, to infufe the fpirit of univerfal be-
nevolence into the hearts of all men—Is is— to
extirpate every vice, that can infeft, or debafe
our nature, and to cultivate every virtue that
can exalt, and adorn it—It is—to give mankind
the ftrongeft motives to promote each other's
happinefs, that the heart of man is capable of
receiving, and confequently — It is carrying the
happinefs of mankind to the higheft pitch, that,
in the nature of things, it is poffible to be carried by any motives.— Thefe virtues, and thefe
motives to virtue, are all deducible from the
doctrines of Chrift; and in a juft proportion, as
thefe motives operate, and thefe virtues are produced, happinefs is the natural, and genuine
effect. The virtues cannot be produced with-

out

out the motives, nor the happinefs without the
virtues.

Whether therefore thefe doctrines are true,
or falfe, the effect of them, if univerfaly and
confiftently obeyed and followed, is certain.   It
is univerfal good-will towards each other, and
univerfal praife and thankfgiving to our Creator.
If the doctrines are true, every man's duty,
and every man's intereft, is concerned to propagate them: but fuppofe them falfe, no man's duty,
and no man's intereft is concerned to refute
them.   For to endeavour to refute them, is, to
endeavour to deftroy the ftrongeft foundation, on
which the order and happinefs of mankind can
be built.   But on what law can any fuch duty
be founded ? — Not on any revealed law of
God—Not on any law of right reafon, for that
leads all men to the greateft happinefs attain-
able.   Neither can it be founded on any law of
truth, that has any fanction to inforce obedience to it—For, if it is a truth, that the ftrongeft
foundation on which the greateft happinefs of
mankind can be built, ought to be deftroyed, it
is a truth, to whofe law general obedience would
be punifhed with general mifery, and general
difobedience rewarded with general happinefs.
As happinefs therefore, in the nature of things,
is

is, superior, and preferable to misery, this supposed falsehood of the Gospel, which in its con-
sequences is productive of the greatest general
happiness, must necessarily, in the nature of
things, be superior, and preferable to this supposed truth.—To conclude.—

Objections may be made to particular points
of the Christian doctrine, arising from ignorance,
prejudice, misunderstanding, and a variety of
other causes; but the general end and tendency
of the whole, no wise man can object to— no
good man will object to— For let the most perfect system of moral laws be devised, that the
wisdom of man can devise, or that the goodness of
man can wish to establish, for the common good
of mankind —every wise man would see, and
every good man would lament the want of proper sanctions and authority to enforce obedience.
But this most perfect system of moral laws, is,
in fact, contained, and taught in the doctrines of
Christ ; and, that very want of sanctions and
authority is amply supplied by the authority of
God himself commanding obedience.

How absurd then for those, who approve the
superstructure, to attack the foundation ? for
those, who revere the virtue, to weaken, and
                                                        destroy

deſtroy the faith, on which alone it can ſtand?
Surely, every wiſe and good man, if he is con-
ſiſtent with his wiſdom and goodneſs, will find
himſelf obliged to join his labours with ours for
the Propagation of the Goſpel, and his prayers with
ours *to the Lord of the Harveſt, that he will ſend
forth the labourers into his harveſt.*

Now to God the Father, &c.

An

An ABSTRACT of the

CHARTER,

And of the Proceedings of the SOCIETY
for the Propagation of the Gospel in
Foreign Parts, from the 20th Day
of *February*, 1761, to the 19th Day
of *February*, 1762.

KING *William* III, of Glorious Memory,
was graciously pleased, on the 16th of
June 1701, *to erect and settle a Corporation with a perpetual Succession, by the Name of*
THE SOCIETY FOR THE PROPAGATION OF
THE GOSPEL IN FOREIGN PARTS ; *for the Receiving, Managing, and Disposing of the Charity
of such Persons as would be induced to extend their
Charity towards* the Maintenance of a Learned
and an Orthodox Clergy, *and the making such
other Provision as might be necessary for the Propagation of the Gospel in Foreign Parts,. upon In-
formation, that in many of our Plantations, Colonies,
and Factories beyond the Seas, the Provision for
Ministers was mean, and many other of our said
Plantations, Colonies, and Factories, were wholly
unprovided of a Maintenance for Ministers, and the
publick Worship of God ; and that, for lack of Support*

port and Maintenance of ſuch, many of his loving Subjects wanted the Adminiſtration of God's Word and Sacraments, and ſeemed to be abandoned to Atheiſm and Infidelity, and others of them to Popiſh Superſtition and Idolatry.

This Society was compoſed, by the Charter, of the Chief Prelates and Dignitaries of the Church, and of ſeveral other Lords, and eminent Perſons in the State, with a Power to elect ſuch others to be Members of the Corporation, as they, or the major Part of them, ſhould think beneficial to their charitable deſigns; and they immediately applied themſelves with great Zeal and Alacrity to the good Work; and after adjuſting Preliminaries in the Choice of Officers, and ſettling ſtanding Orders and Rules for their more regular Proceeding, they ſubſcribed every one of them according to their ſeveral Ranks and Diſpoſitions, an Annual Sum to be paid to their Treaſurer, for the general Uſes of the Society; and choſe new Members, and gave out Deputations according to the Powers in the Charter, to receive and collect the Donations of all charitable and well-diſpoſed Perſons towards this moſt pious Deſign: And thro' an eſpecial Bleſſing, *this Work of the Lord hath hitherto proſpered in their Hands.* Many more than One Hundred Thouſand of our own People, Infants and Adults, and many Thouſands of *Indians* and *Negroes* have been inſtructed and baptized into the true Faith of our Lord Jeſus Chriſt; and more than One Hundred and Thirty Thouſand Volumes of Bibles and Common Prayer Books,

with

with other Books of Devotion and Inftruction, together with an innumerable Quantity of pious fmall Tracts, have been difperfed in Foreign Parts; and there is now a very hopeful and improving Appearance of Religion in the publick Worfhip of God, according to the Liturgy of the Church of *England,* in a great Number of Churches in our Plantations in *America,* by the Means, and through the Procurement of this Corporation.

The Charter directs the Society to give an Annual Account to the Lord High Chancellor, the Lord Chief Juftice of the *King's Bench,* and the Lord Chief Juftice of the *Common Pleas,* of the feveral Sums of Money by them received, and laid out, and of the Management and Difpofition of the Revenues of the Corporation : This is punctually done, and the Society annually makes publick an Abftract of them, and their Proceedings. Therefore the Society now, in the firft Place, acknowledge the Receipt, and return their moft hearty Thanks for the particular Benefactions of the Year 1761, *viz.*

	l.	*s.*	*d.*
To a Perfon unknown, by Mr. *Gell,* ———	1	16	0
For a Legacy of *Vigerus Edwards,* Efq; being one Year's Subfcription, — ———	2	0	0
To *William Bury,* Efq; by the Lord Bifhop of *Waterford,* — —	10	10	0
For a Legacy of the Rev. Dr. *Knatchbull,* by the Rev. Dr. *Dickens,* Prebendary of *Durham,* —— —— —	25	0	0

D To

To a Perſon unknown, by Sir *Thomas Harriſon*,	1	1	0
To a Perſon unknown, by the Lord Biſhop of *Saliſbury*,	21	0	0
To Mr. *Woodrooffe*,	2	2	0
To a Perſon unknown, by the Rev. Mr. *Bouchery*,	0	10	6
To a Perſon unknown,	1	1	0
To a Lady unknown, by Major General *Hudſon*,	2	2	0
To the Rev. Mr. *Leland*, of *Eaſt Dean* in *Suſſex*,	2	2	0
To *C. H.* by the Rev. Mr. *Warren*,	5	5	0
To the Rev. Mr. *Falkner*, of *Well* in *Lincoln-ſhire*, by the Rev. Mr. *Broughton*,	1	1	0
To the Rev. Dr. *Hawtry*, Sub-dean of *Exeter*,	4	4	0
To Mrs. *Ann Maynard*, by *Henry Hoare*, Eſq; and Co.	10	10	0
To the Rev. Mr. *Hughes*, of *Ruthen*, by the Rev. Mr. *Green*,	1	1	0
To Lady *S.* by Mr. *Allen*,	1	1	0
To the Rev. the Dean of *Bangor*,	1	1	0
To the Rev. Mr. *Hughes*, Rector of *Llanfwroy* in *Denbighſhire*,	1	1	0
To a Perſon deſiring to be unknown, by his Grace the Lord Archbiſhop of *Canterbury*,	5	8	0
To a worthy Perſon of *Briſtol*, by the Rev. Mr. *Taylor*, Miniſter of *Clifton*,	5	5	0
To a Gentlewoman, by the Rev. Mr. *Land*,—	1	1	0
To Mrs. *Mary Jodrell*,	1	1	0
To Lady *Palmer*,	1	1	0
To Mrs. *Harding*.	1	1	0
To a Lady unknown, by the Rev. Mr. *Fenwick*,	1	1	0
To a Perſon unknown, by ditto,	1	1	0
To Mrs. *Kelſey*, by the Rev. Mr. *Berriman*, —	0	10	6

To

To Mrs. *Katherine Kelſey*, by ditto, ——	1	1	0
To Mrs. *Frances Peirce*, by ditto, ————	2	2	0
To Mrs. *Mary Berriman*, by ditto, ——	2	2	0
To ſeveral worthy Perſons in and about the City of *York*, by the Rev. the Dean of *York*, —— —— ——	33	4	0
For a Legacy left to the Society by the Laſt Will of Mrs. *Mary Mence*, late of the Pariſh of *Stock* in the County of *Worceſter*,	100	0	0
To two Ladies deſiring to be unknown, ——	3	3	0
To a Perſon unknown, by the Dean of *York*,	10	0	0
To Mrs. *Margaret Floyer*, of *Dorcheſter*, by the Hands of Mr. *Peter Campbell*, ——	10	0	0
To a Perſon unknown, by Mr. *Lane*, ——	2	2	0
To the Rev. Mr. *Edward Wilſon*, of *Suſſex*,	10	0	0
For a Legacy of Dr. *Stephen Hales*, by the Rev. Mr. *Johnſon* and *Sarah Margaretta* his Wife, Executors, ——	100	0	0
For a Legacy of the Rev. Mr. *Caſtelman*, by the Hon. Mrs. *Caſtelman* his Widow and Executrix, —— —— ——	50	0	0
To Lady *Curzon*, —— ——	5	5	0
To the Right Hon. Lord Viſcount *Folkeſton*,—	10	10	0
To *Charles Jennens*, Eſq; of *Gopſal*, *Leiceſter-ſhire*, by Mr. *John Hetherington*, —— ——	21	0	0
To the Rev. Mr. *Harvey*, of *Laws Hill, Suffolk*,	2	2	0
To Mrs. *Suſan Matthew*, by the Rev. Mr. *Reyner*, —— —— ——	1	1	0
To Mrs. *Norris*, of *Great Hitchingham* in *Norfolk*, by Mr. *White*, — —	5	5	0
To *E. W. D.* —— —— —	10	10	0

D 2   To

To Mrs. *Jodrell*, of *Chefter*, ——— —	1	1	0
For a Legacy of Mrs. *Ruffel*, by her Executor *Jofeph Brook*, Efq; — ———	20	0	0
To a Clergyman in the Eaft of *Suffex*, by the Rev. Mr. *Edward Wilfon*, ——— ——	1	1	0
To *E. P.* ——— ——— — —	2	2	0
To a Lady unknown, by Meff. *John* and *Chriftopher Heath*, ——— — ——	5	5	0
To Mrs. *Rachael Rectrick*, — — —	1	1	0
For a Legacy of the late Lord Bifhop of *London* Dr. *Sherlock*, paid by his Lordfhip's Executors, ——— — —	200	0	0
For a Legacy of the Rev. Mr. *Spateman*, Vicar of *Chifwick*, paid by his Executrix Mrs. *Watfon*, ——— ——— ———	21	0	0
To *D. B.* ——— ——— ———	3	3	0
To Mrs. *Percival*, of *Southampton*, by Mr. *Keckwich*, ——— ——— ——	2	2	0
To *Francis Turner Blythe*, Efq; Executor of Mrs. *Jane Jenks*, late of *Shrewfbury*, Widow, by Mr. *John Afhby*, ——— —	100	0	0
To a Gentlewoman unknown, by the Rev. Dr. *Halifax*, ——— ——— ——	1	1	0
To *John Jex*, Efq; and the Rev. Mr. *Belward*, Executors of Mr. *Thomas Mund*, late of *Lowftoffe* in *Suffolk*, ——— ——	400	0	0
To Mrs. *Hindmarch*, of *Newcaftle*, ———	2	2	0
To the Executor of Mrs. *Ingram*, ———	1	0	0
For a Legacy of Mrs. *Eliz. Woodward*, by Mrs. *Lois Andrews* her Executrix, ———	50	0	0

To

To the Rev Dr. *Troughear,* and his Friends, *viz.*

To the Rev. Dr. *Thoughear*,	—	1	1	0		
To Mrs. *Cordelia Holmes*,	——	1	1	0		
To a pious Widow,	——	0	10	6		
To Sir *John Oglander*, Bart.	——	1	1	0		
To Sir *Edward Worsley*, Knt.	—	1	1	0		
To *David Urry*, Esq;	——	1	1	0		
To *George Bockland*, Esq;	——	1	1	0		
To *Barn. Ev. Leigh*, Esq;	——	1	1	0		
To Mr. *Robert Worsley*,	——	0	10	6		
To Mr. *White*, of *Newport*,	—	0	10	6	16	5 6
To Mr. *Clark*,	——	0	10	6		
To Mr. *Leigh*, of *Thorley*,	——	0	10	6		
To the Rev. Mr. *Atkinson*,	——	1	1	0		
To the Rev. Mr. *Bracon*,	——	1	1	0		
To the Rev. Mr. *Curm*,	——	1	1	0		
To the Rev. Mr. *Palmer*,	——	1	1	0		
To the Rev. Mr. *Walton*,	——	1	1	0		
To Collection in *Newport* and *Northwood*, —— ——		1	1	0		
To a Person unknown, by Mr. *Godfrey Lee Farrant*, —— ——			5	5 0		
For a Legacy of Mrs. *Mary Berriman* in *East India* Annuities, transferred by her Executors, — — — —			100	0 0		
For a Legacy of the Rev. Dr. *Samuel Holcombe*, in Old *South-Sea* Annuities, transferred by his Executors, ——			100	0 0		
To *Paul Fisher*, Esq; near *Bristol*, by Mr. *Lawrence Cole*, — —			5	5 0		
To Mrs. *Elwes* of *Chiswick*, by Mr. *Walter Dicker*, — — —			100	0 0		

To

To a Person unknown, by _Samuel Clark_, Efq;	1	1	0
To the Hon. Mrs. _Shirley_, — — •	5	5	0
To Mrs. _Pudner_, by the Rev. Mr. Archd._Head_,	2	2	0
To a Person unknown, by ditto, ——	2	2	0
To a Clergyman of _Devonshire_, by the Rev. Mr. _Perfect_ of _Rochester_, ——	0	5	0
To Mrs. _Toogood_ of _Briftol_, by the Rev. the Dean of _Glocefter_, —— ——	1	1	0
To _Humph. Fitfherbert_, Efq; by ditto, —	2	2	0
To Mrs. _Patience Jones_, by ditto, ——	1	1	0
To a Person unknown, by Mr. _John Withers_,	7	7	0
To a Person unknown, by the Rev. Mr. _John Taylor_, Minister of the _Hotwell_ Chapel, _Briftol_, —— ——	5	5	0
To Mrs. _Lucy Ofborn_, of _Seething_ in _Norfolk_, by the Rev. Mr. _Broughton_, —— —	2	2	0
To the Rev. Mr. Subdean _Hawtry_, ——	4	4	0
To a Gentleman of _Lowth_ in _Lincolnfhire_, by his Friend in _London_, —— ——	2	2	0
To Mrs. _Sarah Carte_, of _Carlton_, _Leicefterfhire_, by the Rev. Mr. _Wefton_, ——	1	1	0
To the Rev. Mr. _Allen_, of _Blundefton_ in _Suffolk_, by Mr. _Whifton_, —— ——	2	10	6
To a Person unknown, by the Rev. Mr._Archer_,	1	11	6
To the Rev. Mr. _Wheeler_, of _Leet_ in _Nottinghamfhire_, —— ——	3	3	0
To a Gentlewoman unknown, by the Rev. Mr. _Land_, —— ——	1	1	0
To Mrs. _Dolliffe_, by the Rev. Dr. _Crufius_, —	2	2	0
To Mr. _Parker_, by the Rev. Mr. _Land_, ——	1	1	0
Total	**1677**	**7**	**6**

Thefe Benefactions, together with Three Pounds three Shillings, paid at Entrance of new Members, amounting to the Sum of One thoufand Six Hundred and Eighty Pounds, Ten Shillings, and Six Pence, are all the Benefactions to the Society in the Year 1761; all which, and a much larger Sum, amounting in the Whole to the Sum of Four Thoufand Nine Hundred Fifty Four Pounds, Eight Shillings, and Three Pence, has been expended in Salaries, and other incidental Charges, &c. and for Books fent by the Society to *North America.*

Alfo the Society return their Thanks for 6 Copies of, Lectures on the Principles of the Chriftian Religion; a Prefent from the Author *Jofeph Parfons,* M. A. For 100 Copies of Bifhop *Sherlock*'s 3d and 4th Volumes of Sermons. As alfo for 50 Copies of, *Orbis Eruditi Literatura è Charactere Samaritico deducta*; by *Charles Morton,* M.D. to be fent to the Society's Miffionaries, whofe Names, together with thofe of the Society's Catechifts and School-mafters, with their refpective Salaries, are as follow:

Newfoundland.	Annual Salaries.
	l.
1 Mr. *Langman,* Miffionary at St. *John's* Town,	50
2 Mr. ———, Miffionary at *Trinity Bay,*	50

Nova Scotia.	
3 Mr. *Wood,* Miffionary to the *Englifh,*	70

4 Mr.

4 Mr. *Breynton*, Missionary to the *English*,—70
5 Mr. *Moreau*, Missionary to the *French*, — 70
6 Mr. *Buchanan*, Schoolmaster to the *English*, 15
7 Mr. *Bailley*, Schoolmaster to the *French*,— 15
8 Mr. *Bennet*, Itinerant Missionary at *Lu-*} 70
     nenburg,

New England.

9 Mr. *Browne*, Missionary at *Newport* in } 50
     Rhode Island,
10 Mr. *Fayerweather*, Missionary at *Nara-*} 50
     ganset,
11 Mr. *Bass*, Missionary at *Newbury*, —— 50
12 Mr. *Usher*, Missionary at *Bristol*, —— 60
13 Dr. *Cutler*, Missionary at *Christ Church* } 70
     in *Boston*,
14 Mr. *Bours*, Missionary at *Marblehead*, — 50
15 Mr. *Winslow*, Missionary at *Stratford*, — 50
16 Mr. *Newton*, Missionary at *Ripton*, —— 30
17 Mr. *Lamson*, Missionary at *Fairfield*, —— 50
18 Mr. *Dibblee*, Missionary at *Stamford*,—— 50
19 Mr. *Browne*, Missionary at *Portsmouth* in } 60
     New Hampshire, —— —
—————For officiating at *Kittery*, —— 15
20 Mr. *Matthew Graves*, Missionary at *New* } 60
     London,
21 Mr. *Beach*, Missionary at *Newtown*, —— 50
22 Mr. *John Graves*, Missionary at *Providence*, 50
23 Mr. *Taylor*, Schoolmaster at *Providence*,— 10
24 Mr. *Macgilchrist*, Missionary at *Salem*, — 50
25 Mr. *Punderson*, Itinerant Missionary in } 50
     Connecticut,

                        26 Mr.

26 Mr. *Hutchinson*, Schoolmaster at *North-Groton*, —— —— —} 5

27 Mr. *Thompson*, Missionary at *Scituate*,—— 50

28 Mr. *Gibbs*, Missionary at *Simsbury*, —— 30

29 Mr. *Mansfield*, Missionary at *Derby*, —— 30

30 Mr. *Leaming*, Missionary at *Norwalk*, — 50

31 Dr. *Miller*, Missionary at *Braintree*, —— 60

32 Mr. *Davies*, Itinerant Missionary in *Lich-field* County, and Parts adjacent,——}30

33 Mr. *Bailey*, Itinerant Missionary on the Eastern Frontiers of *Massachuset's Bay*, }50

34 Mr. *Camp*, Missionary to *Middleton* and *Wallingford*, —— —— }20

35 Mr. *Scovil*, Missionary to *Waterbury* and *Northbury* in *Connecticut*, —— }20

36 Mr. *Peters*, Missionary at *Hebron*, —— 20

37 Mr. *Apthorp*, Missionary at *Cambridge*,— 50

38 Mr. *Andrews*, Missionary at *Wallingford*,&c.20

39 Mr. *Beardslee*, Missionary at *Groton*,&c:— 30

New York.

40 Mr. *Seabury*, junior, Missionary at *Jamaica* Town in *Long Island*, —— ——}50

41 Mr. *Seabury*, Missionary at *Hemstead* in *Long Island*, —— ——}50

42 Mr. —— Missionary at *Rye*, —— 50

43 Mr. *Timothy Wetmore*, Schoolmaster at *Rye*, 10

44 Mr. *Charlton*, Missionary at *Staten Island*, 50

45 Mr. —— Schoolmaster at *Staten Island*, 15

46 Mr. *Milner*, Missionary at *West Chester*,— 50

47 Mr. —— Schoolmaster at *West Chester*,— 10

48 Mr. *Houdin*, Missionary at *New Rochelle*, . 50

E. 49 Mr.

49 Mr. *Ogilvie*, Miſſionary at *Albany*, and
   to the *Mohock Indians*, ⎯⎯ } 50

50 Mr. *Oël*, Aſſiſtant to Mr. *Ogilvie* among
   the *Indians*, ⎯⎯ ⎯⎯} 10

51 *Paulus*, a *Mohock*, Schoolmaſter to the
   Indians, ⎯⎯ ⎯⎯ } 7 10

52 Mr. *Lyons*, Miſſionary at *Brookhaven* in
   Long Iſland, ⎯⎯ ⎯⎯} 50

53 Mr. *Watkins*, Miſſionary at *Newburgh*,⎯ 30

54 Mr. *Auchmuty*, Catechiſt to the Negroes
   at *New York*, ⎯⎯ ⎯⎯} 50

55 Mr. *Hildreth*, Schoolmaſter at *New York*, 15

New Jerſey.

56 Mr. *Chandler*, Miſſionary at *Elizabeth
   Town* and *Woodbridge*, ⎯⎯ } 50

57 Mr. *Palmer*, Miſſionary at *Amboy*, ⎯⎯ 60

58 Mr. *Campbell*, Miſſionary at *Burlington*,⎯ 60

59 Mr. *Cooke*, Miſſionary in *Monmouth County*, 60

60 Mr. ⎯⎯ Schoolmaſter at *Shrewſbury*, 10

61 Mr. *Browne*, Miſſionary at *Newarke*,⎯⎯ 50

62 Mr. *Mackean*, Miſſionary at *New Brunſ-
   wicke*, ⎯⎯ ⎯⎯ } 50

63 Mr. ⎯⎯ Itinerant Miſſionary at *New
   Jerſey*, ⎯⎯ ⎯⎯ } 50

64 Mr. ⎯⎯ Schoolmaſter at *Second River*, 10

65 Mr. *Morton*, Itinerant Miſſionary in the
   North-Weſtern Frontier of *New Jerſey*,} 50

Pennſylvania.

66 Mr. *Roſs*, Miſſionary at *Newcaſtle*, ⎯⎯ 60

67 Mr.

67 Mr. *Reading*, Miffionary at *Apoquini-*⎤
     minck,   ——   ——⎦60

68 Mr. *Craig*, Miffionary at *Chefter*, —— 60

69 Mr. *Neill*, Miffionary at *Oxford*, —— 60

70 Mr. *Currie*, Miffionary at *Radnor*, —— 60

71 Mr. *Inglis*, Miffionary at *Dover*, —— 50

72 Mr. *Barton*, Itinerant Miffionary at *Lan-*⎤
     cafter,   ——   ——⎦50

73 Mr. *Sturgeon*, Catechift to the Negroes⎰
     in *Philadelphia*,   —— ——⎰50

74 Mr. *Thompfon*, Itinerant Miffionary in the⎰
     Counties of *York* and *Cumberland*, ——⎰50

North Carolina.

75 Mr. *Moir*, Itinerant Miffionary, —— 50

76 Mr. *Earl*, Miffionary at St. *Paul's Pa-*⎰
     rifh, *Chowan County*,   ——⎰50

77 Mr. *Stewart*, Miffionary at St. *Thomas's*⎰
     Bath Town.   ——   ——⎰50

78 Mr. *Read*, Miffionary in *Craven County*,— 50

79 Mr. *Mackdowell*, Miffionary at *Brunfwick*, 50

South Carolina.

80 Mr. *Garden*, Miffionary at *St. Thomas's*, 30

81 Mr. *Durand*, Miffionary at *St. John's* in⎰
     Berkley County,   ——⎰30

82 Mr. *Harrifon*, Miffionary at *St. James's*⎰
     Goofe-Creek,   —— ——⎰30

83 Mr. *Baron*, Miffionary at *St. Bartholo-*⎰
     mew's,   ——   ——⎰30

Georgia.

84 Mr. *Duncanson*, Missionary at *Savannah*,   50

Bahama Islands.

85 Mr. *Carter*, Missionary,   ——   60
——— as Schoolmaster,   ——   10

Total £ 3727 10 0

Barbadoes.

86 Mr. *Falcon*, Schoolmaster at *Codrington* College,   —— } 100

87 Mr. *Duke*, Usher of the School, and Catechist to the Negroes,   —— } 70

N. B These two Salaries are paid out of the Produce of the Plantation.

The Society allow Ten Pounds Worth of Books to each Mission for a Library, and Five Pounds Worth of pious small Tracts to every new Missionary, to be distributed among their Parishioners; and other Parcels of Books, as Occasion offers, and the Society find them wanting. And the Society have received the following Accounts of their pious Labours in the Year 1761.

Newfoundland.

The Rev. Mr. *Langman*, the Society's Missionary at St. *John's Town in Newfoundland*, in his Letter dated *June* 23, 1761, acquaints the Society, that he arrived safe at his Mission on *May* 28, and purposed visiting the Southern Harbours,

bours, which he could not vifit laft Summer, but was afraid he fhould not be able to vifit any of the Northern Harbours, as the Summers in thofe Parts are very fhort ; however, promifes to vifit them all as often as he can, confiftent with his more immediate Duty at St. *John's*, and to follow all fuch Directions as the Society fhall give him. He writes, That the new Church at St. *John's* was almoft finifhed ; which would render their affembling for Divine Worfhip more commodious than heretofore. In another Letter, dated *Nov.* 4, 1761, he writes, That he vifited in *Auguft* laft, *Bay Bulls* and *Whitlafs Bay*, where he ftaid ten Days : That in the Harbour of *Bay Bulls* are 37 Families of *Irifh* Papifts, and 8 of Proteftants ; in all about 230 Souls. He baptized 4 of the Proteftants Children ; but could not perfuade the Papifts to have theirs baptized by him. In *Whitlafs Bay* are 11 poor Families, almoft all *Irifh Roman* Catholics, as they are in the reft of the Harbours and Bays of this Ifland, where the few Proteftants there are, are in Danger even of their Lives ; fo that, were they not fomewhat reftrained by the Fear of the Civil Power, there would be no tolerable living in the Ifland. He purpofes, God willing, next Summer to vifit Harbour *Grace*, and fome Places 30 or 40 Miles Northward. By Mr. *Langman's Notitia Parcchialis* it appears, that the Number of Souls in the Limits of St. *John's Town*, as taken by Survey laft Winter, was as follows ; of *Englifh* Men, Women, and Children, 557 ; of
Irifh

Irish Roman Catholics 629. In all 1186. In the laſt Year he had baptized 16, two of which were Adults : Buried 42. His regular Communicants are 30. He begs a further Supply of Bibles, Common-Prayer Books, and other good Books; which will be forwarded the firſt Opportunity.

The Society have not been able this Year to find a proper Perſon for Miſſionary to *Trinity Bay*, in the room of Mr. *Lindſay* ; but hope to ſend one ſoon.

Nova Scotia.

In Conſequence of ſeveral Letters laid before the Society by *John Pownal*, Eſq; Secretary to the Board of Trade; ſetting forth the Neceſſity of eſtabliſhing a new Miſſion in *Nova Scotia*, amongſt the *German* Settlers at *Lunenburg* and the Parts adjacent, who underſtand *Engliſh* very well, and are deſirous of uniting themſelves and their Children (of whom the latter now ſcarce ſpeak any other Language but *Engliſh*) into one Congregation, under the Church of *England* Government ; the Society have appointed the Rev. Mr. *Joſeph Bennet*, Itinerant Miſſionary there, who is directed to officiate chiefly at *Lunenburg*, but occaſionally alſo, as need ſhall require, in the ſeveral other Townſhips, which are, or ſhall be, erected in the Province, as the Governor ſhall direct, till the Bounds of his Miſſion are more fully ſettled. Mr. *Bennet* is in the 34th Year of his Age, and is recommended to the Society as a Man of good Temper, Prudence, and Learning, and

and of a fober and pious Converfation, zealous
for the Chriftian Religion, throughly well affected to the prefent Government, and one who has
always conformed to the Doctrine and Difcipline
of the Church of *England.*

New England.

The Rev. Mr. *Fayerweather*, the Society's Miffionary at *Narraganfet*, by his Letter dated *Dec.* 1,
176c, which was laid before the Board *April* 17,
1761, acquaints the Society, That after officiating
a few *Sundays* in the Parifh Church of St. *Paul* in
his new Miffion, he had the Misfortune of fprain-
ing his right Ancle, which till that Time had
confined him in great Pain ; but promifes, upon
his Recovery, to be diligent in the Society's Service, and obey their Injunctions, and to exert
himfelf, to the utmoft of his Srength and Capa-
city, to the Honour of God, and the Propagation
of the Gofpel of our Great Redeemer. By another Letter dated *March* 20, 1761, we learn,
That he is fo far reftored as to go out again, and
promifes to do his utmoft to redeem the loft
Time. He complains, That Quakers, Baptifts,
Fanaticks, Ranters, Deifts, and Infidels, fwarm
in that Part of the World : But in another Letter, dated *Aug.* 1, 1761, writes, That his own
Flock, to his unfpeakable Comfort, increafe in
Number, and, as he judges by the Fruits, grow
in the Graces and Virtues of the Chriftian Life.
He adds, That many good Books are wanted in
the *Narraganfet* County, for the Suppreffing of
Deifin,

Deiſm, Infidelity, and Quakeriſm, which, if ſent
to his Care and Diſpoſal, he promiſes ſhall be di-
ſtributed in a Manner beneficial to his own
People, and to thoſe who diſſent from our Eſtab-
liſhment. Which Requeſt the Society have complied with; and beſides Bibles, Common-Prayer
Books, and many pious ſmall Tracts, have ſent
12 Copies of *Weſt on the Reſurrection*, and *Lyttle-
ton on the Converſion of St. Paul*; and 12 of
Leſlie's ſhort and eaſy Method with the Deiſts.
  The Rev. Mr. *Baſs*, the Society's Miſſionary
at *Newbury*, writes, in his Letters of *Sept.* 29,
1760, and *March* 25, 1761, That his Congregation continues to increaſe, though very ſlowly;
that he has baptized at *Newbury*, within the
Year, 12 Infants, and ſix, together with a Ne-
groWoman and her three Children, at *Hopkinton*;
to which Place he made a Journey toward the
End of the Year 1760, and preached to a conſiderable Congregation, who ſeemed to be earn-
eſtly deſirous of a Miſſionary. He alſo preached,
two or three Months before the Date of his laſt
Letter, at *Amſbury*, five or ſix Miles from *Newbury*, over the River *Merrimack*, to a conſiderable
Number of People in a private Houſe; But they
are preparing to build a Church, and are in
Hopes of the Society's Favours in due Time,
upon Compliance with the Terms required. In
another Letter, dated *Sept.* 29, 1761, he complains, That the Diſſenters, upon his refuſing to
give them Leave to hold their Religious Meet-
ings in his Church, till they could build a Meet-
ing-houſe,

ing-houfe, had forcibly intruded into it; and that thereupon he confulted Governor *Bernard*, who recommended the granting them the Ufe of the Church, upon their difclaiming all Right to it, and difavowing the Force they had ufed. But Mr. *Bafs*, confidering the Church as a Truft committed to him by the Society, earneftly requefts their Directions upon this Head, who have ordered him to follow Governor *Bernard*'s Advice, in permitting the Diffenters to make Ufe of the Church for a limited Time, fuch as the Governor fhall recommend, provided they difclaim all Manner of Right to it, and provided their affembling there does not interfere with the Hours of his performing Divine Service, and other occafional Duties of his Parifh.

The Rev. Mr. *Bours*, the Society's Miffionary at *Marblehead*, in a Letter dated *Aug.* 2, 1761, acquaints them, That the greateft Unanimity reigns amongft the feveral Denominations in that Place: That he has conftantly a full Audience, who are in general devout in their Worfhip, and exemplary in their Lives. From *June* 24, 1760, to *June* 24, 1761, he has baptized 59 Infants. His Communicants are 47.

The Rev. Mr. *Winflow*, the Society's Miffionary at *Stratford*, in his Letters of *Dec.* 29, 1760, and *July* 1, 1761, informs the Society, That within the Year he had baptized 33 White, and 3 Negro Children, and that his Number of Communicants is near 150: That the Church in *Stratford* fupports its Reputation and Influence,

F   and

and gains Strength, notwithſtanding a reſtleſs
Spirit of Oppoſition but too viſible in ſome of
the Diſſenting Teachers of Authority and Influence : But he obſerves, that the Diviſions
among the Diſſenters have unſettled ſo many,
that he doubts not but Numbers will embrace
that Refuge from Confuſion, which our happy
Conſtitution will afford them. This, he ſays,
is manifeſtly the Caſe at *Wallingford*, where the
Church Congregation has ſo far increaſed, that
the People think themſelves in a Condition to
make a ſuitable Proviſion for a deſerving young
Man, who had been ſome Time employed as a
Reader among them. This Gentleman (Mr.
Andrews) has ſince been ſent to *England*, very
ſtrongly recommended to the Society, and being
found worthy, was admitted into Holy Orders,
and received into the Society's Service, as Miſſionary to the People of *Wallingford*, *Cheſhire*,
Meridan, and *North Haven*, who have jointly
contracted to raiſe 50 *l.* Sterling *per Annum*, with
a Houſe and Glebe of 14 Acres for his better
Accommodation.

The Rev. Mr. *Dibblee*, the Society's Miſſionary at *Stamford*, in his Letter dated *March* 25,
1761, returns his hearty Thanks to the Society
for paſt Favours, and promiſes his utmoſt Endeavours to deſerve the Continuance of them by
Diligence and Fidelity. He writes further, That
upon making a Viſit to the People of *Weſt
Cheſter*, (who were at that Time without a Miſſionary) he paid his Reſpects to the worthy Mr.
St.

St. George Talbot, a Gentleman of great Piety, Zeal, and Charity, who, befides the Benefaction to the Church of *Rye*, of 600 *l. New York* Currency, has alfo given a like Sum for the Encouragement of Religion among the poor People of *North Caftle*; a like Benefaction to the Church of *Flufhing* in *Long Ifland*; and (as we learn from another Letter of Mr. *Dibblee's*, dated *Sept.* 29, 1761,) has judged the Church of *Stamford* worthy of his Charity, and made them alfo a free Donation of 600 *l. New York* Currency, to be improved hereafter as the Society fhall direct, or Mr. *Talbot* fhall prefcribe by his Laft Will. Mr. *Dibblee* prays God to reward their generous Benefactor, and hopes himfelf to improve every Encouragement he meets with, by labouring to be as extenfively ufeful as he can. From this worthy Gentleman, the Society have been favoured with a Letter, dated *May* 16, 1761, acknowledging the Honour done him in chofing him a Member of the Society, expreffing his Zeal for true Religion, according to the Doctrine, Worfhip, and Government of our Church; and his earneft Defire to further the noble and charitable Defigns of the Society, by fubmitting what he fhall be able to contribute, to their Direction, for the good of the feveral Churches on which he has beftowed his Charity; fo long, and no longer than they fhall continue to deferve the Society's Notice. Mr. *Dibblee* adds, That his People continue in a peaceable, united State; paying, in general, a due Regard to all

F 2 the

the Offices of Re'igion, in all Parts of his extensive Mission. He writes, That the Dissenters at *Greenwich*, in Concurrence with the Church-People, have requested him to attend Divine Service there on *Sundays*, as often as is consistent with the other Duties of his Cure : Which good Disposition he endeavours to improve, not only by allotting them one *Sunday* in Eight, but also by preaching to them every *Sunday* after Evening Service is over at *Stamford*, so long as he shall be able to attend three Services. The Heads of Families in *Stamford*, *Greenwich*, and the Parishes belonging to them, are 152 ; actual Communicants 53 ; Infants baptized within the Year 56 ; Adults 3.

The Rev. Mr. *John Graves*, the Society's Missionary at *Providence*, in a Letter dated *May* 5, 1761, writes, That his constant Communicants are almost doubled ; and his stated Hearers more than proportionably increased with Persons who practise, as well as profess Religion. As to his particular Charge, he never leaves it, except when he visits his Relations, Spring and Fall, at *New London*. He has kept together, the three last Years, the little Church of *Warwick*, (ten Miles from *Providence*) and given them constant Attendance, Preaching, Administring the Lord's Supper, taking into the Church both Infants and Adults, catechising their Children, visiting their Sick, and burying their Dead. For this extraordinary Attendance on the Church of *Warwick*,

the

the Society have ordered Mr. *John Graves* a Gratuity.

The Rev. Mr. *Beach*, the Society's Miſſionary at *Newtown*, in a Letter dated *Oct.* 14, 1760, rejoices to think, That the War being now happily concluded in that Country, there will, in a ſhort Time, be the beſt Opportunity of propagating the Goſpel among the heathen Natives of that Part of the World, that was ever offered ; as the *French* Prieſts will no longer be able to raiſe Jealouſies amongſt them, and the *Engliſh* will ſoon build new Towns near the *Indian* Settlements, where Miſſionaries may reſide, and enjoy all the Advantages which can be wiſhed for to effect their Converſion. In another Letter, dated *April* 6, 1761, which he apprehends may be the laſt Time of his writing to the Society, he takes Occaſion to return them his hearty Thanks for the charitable Support they have given him for 29 Years, in which he has laboured faithfully to propagate true Religion ; and hopes he has not laboured in vain. The Members of the Church of *England*, he ſays, are increaſed ſince his coming into thoſe Parts, more than ten-fold ; and, which is of greater Importance, their Conduct is, for the moſt part, a Credit to their Profeſſion. Of 800 Members of the Church of *England* in his Cure, 240 are actual Communicants.

The Rev. Mr. *Leaming*, the Society's Miſſionary at *Norwalk*, in his Letter dated *April* 7, 1761, acquaints the Society, That the Church
of

of *Norwalk* is now compleatly finiſhed, and a good Bell purchaſed, of 600 Pounds Weight; and that the Members of the Church give conſtant Attendance on publick Worſhip, and, by their ſerious Behaviour, appear to do it from a Senſe of Duty. By his *Notitia Parochialis* it appears, he had baptized, within the Year, 46 White, and 6 Negro Children, and 1 Adult Negro after proper Inſtruction.

The Rev. Mr. *Palmer*, late the Society's Itinerant Miſſionary in *Litchfield County* and Parts adjacent, is, at his own earneſt Requeſt frequently repeated, removed to the ſettled Miſſion at *Amboy* in *New Jerſey*, he being no longer able to bear the Fatigues of an Itinerant Miſſion; and is ſucceeded by the Rev. Mr. *Davies*, an hopeful young Man, ſtrongly recommended by Dr. *Johnſon*, Mr. *Palmer*, and others, as truly worthy of the Society's Notice and Encouragement.

The Rev. Mr. *Matthew Graves*, the Society's Miſſionary at *New London*, in his Letter dated *Dec.* 13, 1760, acquaints the Society, That the Number of Pews had lately been enlarged, and an handſome Gallery erected in the Church, and yet there is not Room for the Families that frequent it; that his Communicants increaſe, and he had lately baptized an adult Anabaptiſt well prepared, and gained a large growing Family of that Sect, to be of the Number of his Hearers, which he hoped to bring regularly into our Communion; and he bleſſes God that he is beloved

loved by the People of all Denominations, who often attend on his publick Miniftry, and frequent his Houfe, and demonftrate their Good-will to him. In his Letter dated *July* 14, 1761, he laments his bodily Weaknefs and Infirmities ; but bleffes God his Parifhioners increafe amazingly, to whom, he trufts in God, others will be foon joined. In both Letters he applies for a Number of Religious Books, which the Society have readily granted him.

The Rev. Mr. *Bailey*, the Society's Itinerant Miffionary on the Eaftern Frontiers of *Maffachufets Bay*, in his Letter dated *March* 26, 1761, writes, That on his Arrival at *Frankfort*, he was received by the poor Inhabitants of that and the neighbouring Parts, with manifeft Tokens of Satisfaction, who appeared fenfibly affected with the Goodnefs of the Society. He found in the County of *Lincoln*, which contains 1500 Families fcattered over a Country 100 Miles in Length and 60 in Breadth, no Teachers of any Denomination, except a Number of illiterate Exhorters, who ramble about the Country, and do all they can to feduce the People from Order and Decency. The People in thofe Parts, he fays, are a Mixture of feveral Nations, Languages, and Religions ; that however, they are pretty conftant in attending publick Worfhip, and, as foon as the Calamities of War are over, it feems probable that Induftry will increafe, and the People become more fober and virtuous. In his Letter dated *Sept.* 25, 1761, he writes, That he
finds

finds the People more generally diſpoſed to attend Divine Service, and their Demand for his Labours continually increaſing ; but the Country is ſo extenſive, and the Difficulties in Travelling ſo great, that it is impoſſible for one Miſſionary to give proper Attendance. In *George Town*, where he has frequently preached and adminiſtred the Sacrament, the Diſſenters, he thinks, incline ſo much to our Church, that, had they a Miſſionary reſident, they would probably come over to it. *Fort Richmond* is continually increaſing, and the Inhabitants ſo well diſpoſed, that they have ſubſcribed to the Building of a Church, and have hitherto complied with their Engagements to the Society. He obſerves, That *George Town*, *Brunſwick*, *Harpwell*, *Frankfort* or *Pownal Borough*, and *Richmond*, all claim an equal Share in his Services, which obliges him frequently to preach among them at other Times beſides *Sundays*. His Communicants at *George Town* are 17, at *Frankfort* 20. He has baptized within the Year 48 Infants, and 1 Adult. At Mr. *Bailey's* Requeſt, a Number of Common-Prayer Books, Catechiſms, and pious ſmall Tracts, have been ſent to him for the Uſe of the Poor in his Miſſion.

The Rev. Mr. *Peters*, the Society's Miſſionary at *Hebron*, in his Letter dated *April* 13, 1761, expreſſes his grateful Senſe of the Obligations he owes to the Society, and his earneſt Deſire to promote their pious Deſigns by a faithful Diſcharge of his Duty. He writes, That the
Church-

Church-People at *Hebron* are religiously attentive
to his Inftructions, and the Diffenters behave
much better than they ufed to do, and a good
Friendfhip feems to fubfift between him and
their Teachers. He obferves, That his Bufinefs
is great, having only Mr. *Matthew Graves* of
New London within fifty Miles, fo that he is become, by the Importunity of vacant Parifhes, an
Itinerant. His Journeys have been to *Taunton*
100 Miles, to *Sharon* 90, to *Norwich*, *Middle-
town*, *Simfbury*, *Glaffenbury*, *Wallingford*, and
other Places 20 and 30 Miles each. For thefe his
extraordinary Labours, the Society were pleafed
to give Mr. *Peters* a Gratuity.

The Rev. Mr. *Apthorp*, the Society's Miffionary at *Cambridge*, in his Letter dated *Feb.* 14,
1761, acquaints the Society, That they have
been under fome Difficulties in compleating the
Building of their Church, and as it had not yet
been in his Power to be refident at *Cambridge*,
and therefore he had hitherto been of little Service to the Society, he thinks he cannot, with a
fafe Confcience, accept of their Salary for the
Years 1759, and 1760, but begs the Favour of
the Society to grant the Salary for thofe two Years
towards the Building of the Church, which has
been expenfive, and the chief Burthen of it
borne by a very few. As the good People of
Cambridge are likely to incur a confiderable Debt,
which may prevent many of the poorer Sort from
affociating with them, he thinks it will greatly
advance the Intereft of that Miffion to lighten

G   the

the Burthen of the firſt Expence. This Requeſt the Society very readily complied with, and think themſelves greatly obliged to Mr. *Apthorp* for his generous Behaviour on this Occaſion.

New York.

The Rev. Mr. *Seabury*, ſen. the Society's Miſ-ſionary at *Hemſtead* in *Long Iſland*, in his Letter of *Oct.* 21, 1761, writes, That he has had the good Succeſs to bring ſeveral Adults to Baptiſm, who, he hopes, will adorn their Profeſſion. He ob-ſerves, That our Church is well filled both at *Hemſtead* and *Oyſter-Bay*, though the former is ſupplied with an independent Preacher, and in the latter Anabaptiſt and ſeparate Baptiſt Meet-ings are conſtantly held. The Church at *Hunt-ingdon*, where he can attend but ſeldom, is well filled, and the zealous Members always lament their Want of a Miniſter. By his *Notitia Pa-rochialis* it appears, That the Number of Inha-bitants at *Hemſtead* is 5940; of Adults baptized laſt Year 21, one of them a Negro; of Children 109, three of which were Negroes; of Com-municants 72; of Profeſſors of the Church of *England* 750.

Mr. *Timothy Wetmore*, the Society's School-maſter at *Rye*, in a Letter dated *May* 6, 1761, complains, That ſince the Death of his Father they had not been favoured with a Sermon, or had either of the Sacraments adminiſtred in the Pariſh by a Miniſter of the Church of *England*, for ſix or eight Months; that he has preſumed,

at

at the Requeſt of the People in this deſtitute Condition, to read Service every Lord's Day, and upon other convenient Occaſions, which he hopes may, by the Bleſſing of God, tend to keep up a Spirit of Religion, and further the Deſigns of the Society. He obſerves, That the People are conſtant in their Attendance, and decent in their Deportment, and that the Temper of many of the Preſbyterian Congregation, who have now no Miniſter, is ſuch, that if a worthy and acceptable Man was ſettled in that Pariſh, he is much inclined to think they would not call another Preacher, but might many of them be brought into the Church.

The Society have informed the Veſtry, that as ſoon as they ſhall make Application for a Miniſter, and enter into proper Engagements to contribute towards his Support, they intend to appoint a Miſſionary.

The Rev. Mr. *Milner*, the Society's Miſſionary at *Weſt Cheſter*, in his Letter of *October* 3, 1761, acquaints the Society, That after a long and dangerous Paſſage, he arrived at his Miſſion *May* 13, and has ever ſince preached to crowded Audiences. His Miſſion, he ſays, is of large Extent, and he is obliged to attend three Churches, and till Mr. *Houdin* came to *New Rochelle*, officiated there once a Month. One of his Churches is a new Edifice, raiſed by the Generoſity of Col. *Frederic Philips*, who has given to its Service a fine Farm as a Glebe, conſiſting of 200 Acres; upon which he purpoſes to build

G 2   a

a good Houfe for a Minifter. Mr. *Milner* has baptized 43 White Infants, and 4 Adults ; 12 Black Children, and 3 Adults. His Communicants are 16. His Catechumens, he fays, have made a laudable Proficiency, by which Means he hopes his Communicants will increafe.

The Rev. Mr. *Ogilvie*, the Society's Miffionary at *Albany* and to the *Mohcck Indians*, in his Letter dated *October* 14, 1760, informs the Society, That he is obliged to return to *Montreal* for the Winter Seafon, by exprefs Order from Sir *Jeffrey Amherft*, who directed him to procure fome proper Clergyman to fupply his Place at *Albany*, to whom Mr. *Ogilvie* agrees to give the Society's Allowance during his Abfence, which he hopes they will approve of. And it appears by a joint Letter from Dr. *Johnfon*, Dr. *Barclay*, and Mr. *Auchmuty*, that Mr. *Brown*, Chaplain to a Regiment under his Excellency, fupplied Mr. *Ogilvie's* Cure from the *Sunday* before St. *Thomas's Day* 1760, to *November* 1761, when Mr. *Brown* himfelf was ordered on an Expedition. Mr. *Ogilvie*, while he remains at *Montreal*, promifes to do all in his Power to recommend the Church of *England*, and defires a Number of *French* Bibles and Common-Prayer Books, and fome plain Accounts of the Proteftant Religion, written with a Spirit of Moderation and Chriftian Charity. Mr. *Ogilvie* writes farther, That all the Lands upon the Ifland of *Montreal* and Ifle *Jefu* are vefted in the Church ; the Soil is good, and the Country well cultivated ; and fhould they remain

to

to *Great Britain* in a General Peace, out of them might be made a sufficient Provision for a regular and orthodox Clergy.

The Rev. Mr. *Watkins*, the Society's Missionary at *Newburgh*, in a Letter dated *June* 24, 1761, complains, That through the extraordinary Fatigues which he has endured in the Cold and Storms for 16 Years, (riding more than 2000 Miles a Year) his Constitution is much impaired, so that he apprehends he shall not be able to endure so much Fatigue for the Time to come in such a cold Climate, being exceedingly troubled with the Rheumatism. The Society have agreed to remove Mr. *Watkins* to a warmer Climate, as soon as conveniently may be, on account of his long Services. From the 18th of *November* 1760, to the Date of this Letter, he had baptized 23 White Children, and 3 Adults, educated in the Principles of Quakerism. He has baptized since he came to his Mission 727. His Communicants are 90.

The Rev. Mr. *Auchmuty*, the Society's Catechist to the Negroes in the City of *New York*, in his Letter dated *May* 2, 1761, gives an Account, That he had baptized 5 Negroes and 2 Mulatto Adults, after proper Instruction, and 87 Infants, since the Month of *June* 1760 ; and that he had lately had a considerable Increase of young Black Catechumens, many of whom promise very well, and he trusts in God will be exemplary in their Behaviour, and a Credit to our most Holy Religion. In another Letter, dated *Sept.* 19, 1761, he he acquaints the Society, That ſince his laſt Account he has had an Addition of young Catechumens from the Negro School. This School, he ſays, was begun at the Expence of the Aſſociates of Dr. *Bray*, and opened *Sept.* 22, 1760, and, in a little more than four Months, was compleatly full, and ſo continues. The Number is limited to 30, though double that Number have requeſted to be admitted, the Neceſſity and Uſefulneſs of ſuch a School being already ſeen' by many pious Owners of young Slaves. Mr. *Auchmuty* ſays, He frequently viſits the School, hears the Scholars read, ſay their Prayers, *&c.* that they attend his Lectures on the Lord's Day, when he catechiſes them and the Adults together, and is very ſanguine in his Expectations from this little Flock, ſo early inſtructed in the great and important Doctrines of our Holy Religion, and taught their Duty to God and Man. Since his laſt he has baptized 39 Negro Children, and 4 Adults, and has ſeveral others preparing for Baptiſm, and 2 Men for the Holy Communion.

New Jerſey.

The Rev. Mr. *Chandler*, the Society's Miſſionary at *Elizabeth Town* and *Woodbridge*, in his Letter dated *April* 6, 1761, laments the Loſs the Church there ſuſtained by the Removal of Mr. *Bernard* to the Government of *New England*, where he doubts not but his Influence and good Example will be of great Service. He obſerves, That at preſent a general Harmony and good
Underſtanding

Underftanding fubfifts between the Church and
the Diffenters in *New Jerfey*; that the Difputes
between them having for fome Time fubfided,
Candour, Moderation and Charity feem to have
been ftudied, or at leaft affected, on both Sides.
The Diffenters are become fo charitable as to
think there is no material Difference between
them and us; and fuch is the Moderation of
fome Church-men, as to return the Compliment
in their Opinion of the Diffenters. Mr. *Chandler*
continues to do Duty at *Woodbridge*, as far as is
confiftent with his Obligations at *Elizabeth Town*,
and adminifters the holy Communion there three
Times in a Year, *viz.* on the *Sundays* fucceeding
the three great Feftivals. In the preceding Half
Year he had baptized 1 Adult and 29 Infants.
He has had 6 new Communicants this Year;
but as many Perfons, otherwife of unblameable
Lives, continue to be backward in coming to the
holy Communion, notwithftanding his Endeavours, he begs a Number of *The Reafonable
Communicant*, which were fent him accord-
ingly.

The Rev. Mr. *Morton*, the Society's Itinerant
Miffionary on the North-Weftern Frontiers of
New Jerfey, in his Letter dated *July* 1, 1761,
obferves, That the People of *Amwell* and *Ring-
wood* have faithfully difcharged their Obligations
to the Society, having purchafed for the Ufe of
their Miffionary, 50 Acres of good Land, for
which they paid 210 *l.* and are now building a
Houfe for him, which will coft 200 *l.* more;
and

and therefore hopes their Zeal will be rewarded with a Continuance of the Society's Favour. He generally preaches to very large Audiences, and extends his Labours as far as possibly he can. His Communicants at *Easter* last were only 5, the People having been taught by Dissenting Ministers, that they must arrive at almost a State of Perfection before they can be worthy Partakers of that holy Sacrament. He says, He has laboured to set them right in this Matter, and hopes for an Increase of his Communicants. He has baptized in one Year 141. Some Common-Prayer Books, *Lewis*'s Catechisms, and pious Tracts, desired by Mr. *Morton*, are ordered to be sent him by the first Opportunity.

The Rev. Mr. *Mackean*, the Society's Missionary at *New Brunswick*, acquaints the Society, in a Letter dated *October* 5, 1761, That *Spotswood* is more flourishing than ever, so that they have been forced to erect a Gallery in the Church to contain the Numbers usually assembling. The only Thing he mentions, relating to the Church of *Brunswick*, is the obtaining a Charter, under the Title of, *The Rector, Church-wardens, and Vestrymen of Christ Church in New Brunswick*, enabling them to hold Lands, &c. &c. The Right of Presentation is to be in the Society, so long as they please to continue their Bounty ; afterwards in the Church-wardens and Vestry-men. The Rector is to be licensed by the Lord Bishop of *London*, or such other as shall preside over the *American* Churches. In the last Half Year Mr. *Mackean*

Mackean has baptized 19 White Children, and 2 Adults; 4 Black Children, and 1 Adult. The Number of his Communicants at *New Brunf-wick* is decreafed by Removals: At *Spotfwood* he had lately 12 Communicants.

Penfilvania.

The Rev. Mr. *Reading*, the Society's Miffio-nary at *Apoquiniminck*, with his Letter of *June* 25, 1761, tranfmits to the Society 6 *l.* Sterling, being the Legacy of Mrs. *Rebecca Dyre*, to pur-chafe fuch a Piece of Plate as the Society fhall think proper to be ufed at the Adminiftration of the Lord's Supper in the Church of *Apoquini-minck.* His Church, he fays, is already furnifh-ed with a Silver Cup, the Gift of Queen *Anne*; but has neither Paten nor Chalice, properly fo called; he therefore propofes, that fuch a fmall Chalice and Paten may be purchafed as the faid Legacy will allow, with this Infcription; " The " Gift of Mrs. *Rebecca Dyre*, late of *Newcaftle* " *County*, to the Epifcopal Congregation at *Apo-* " *quiniminck.*" Which Propofal the Society readily complied with. Mr. *Reading* has bap-tized, from *Oct.* 1760, to the Date of this, 1 Adult, and 73 Infants, 8 of which were Ne-groes. His Communicants are 63.

The Rev. Mr. *Neill*, the Society's Miffionary at *Oxford*, in a Letter dated *June* 8, 1761, ac-quaints the Society, That he has recovered his Health, and has the Pleafure to fee, that his En-deavours are not thrown away upon the poor

People in his Miffion, but that, by the Bleffing
of Heaven they are growing more numerous and
more fettled in their Principles every Day. He
complains, That many attend Divine Service,
who have not been baptized, and think it a Matter of Indifference, whether they are baptized or
not ; that he has reclaimed fome of thefe, and
hopes to reclaim more. Mr. *Neill* officiated laft
Summer the *Sunday* Evenings in *German Town*,
where the rifing Generation of the *Dutch*, who
underftand *English*, are well affected to the
Church of *England*. He takes Notice how much
the Clergy in general think themfelves obliged to
his Grace the Archbifhop of *Canterbury*, for his
great Pains, Condefcenfion, and Kindnefs, in vin-
dicating them from the Calumnies of Mr. *Mac-
clenaghan* ; upon which they have drawn up an
Addrefs to his Grace, which he hopes will come
fafe to hand.

The Rev. Mr. *Barton*, the Society's Itinerant
Miffionary at *Lancafter*, &c. in his Letter dated
July 6, 1761, excufes himfelf for not fending a
Notitia Parochialis, exactly correfpondent to the
Scheme prefcribed by the Society, which he has
never been able to do ; but has not, to his Knowledge, omitted any material Particular, which
the Circumftances of the Country would permit
him to be acquainted with : A Country, where
there are no ftated Parifhes, and where fome
Miffions extend into two or more Counties, often
making a Circuit of 100 Miles ; and therefore it
muft be next to impoffible to tell what Number
of

of Inhabitants fuch a Territory may contain. In the County of *Lancafter*, which is but Part of his Miffion, he is told there are 32 Townfhips, producing each about 150 Taxables, which, allowing five to a Family, amounts to 24,000. Of thefe, about 1 in 30 is fuppofed to be of the Church of *England*; the reft are Diffenters of every Sort in Chriftendom. Heathens he knows of none among them, except a few *Indians*, who feel and own the Being of a God, and an all-ruling Providence, and, he hopes, will in Time be brought to fee the Neceffity of a Revelation, and embrace Chriftianity. Infidels, avowedly fuch, he has none in his Miffion, but has many pious People in it, as well as many Gainfayers. However, the remarkable Zeal which appears in his Congregations affords him the higheft Joy. In *Lancafter*, the People belonging to the Church, few in Number, and of contracted Fortunes, have raifed a confiderable Sum to build a Steeple, erect Galleries, purchafe a Bell, and finifh the Stone Wall round the Grave-Yard. The poor People in *Pequea* and *Caernarvon* have built two decent Stone Churches, without the leaft Affiftance from the Publick, many Perfons, who were contented to dwell in the meaneft Huts, contributing handfomely to this good Work. Mr. *Barton* has baptized in the laft Half Year 37 Infants, 3 of which were Black. His Communicants at *Eafter* were 85. He has been twice this Summer to vifit *Reading*, where there are a few *Englifh* Families well affected to our Church, as there are alfo

fcattered

scattered here and there in other Parts of the Country, from whom he has frequent Applications, and is determined, as far as the Duties of his extensive Mission will permit, to embrace every Circumstance that promises Succefs to the Caufe of True Religion, and the Advancement of the Church of *England.*

North Carolina.

The Rev. Mr. *Stewart,* the Society's Missionary at St. *Thomas's Bath Town,* in his Letter dated *October* 10, 1760, writes, That in the preceding Half-Year he had baptized in his Mission 82 White Infants, and 13 Black; of Adults, 2 White Men, (1 by Immersion) and 5 Negroes, and his actual Communicants 96. Besides, Mr. *Stewart* visited *Currituck* and *Woodstock* Chapels in *Hyde County,* where they have no resident Minister, and baptized there 46 White, and 9 Black Infants, and preached to two large Congregations. So that Mr. *Stewart's* Return for the whole Year is 249 White, and 48 Black Infants; 4 White, and 14 Black Adults baptized, and 235 actual Communicants. Mr. *Stewart,* when he mentions baptizing a Perfon by Immersion, would be forry to have it thought Affectation of Singularity in him; and affures the Society, he did it only to keep People from falling off from the Church. That Province, he obferves, has of late Years been over-run with a People, who, at first, called themfelves Anabaptists; but who, refining upon that Scheme, have run into so many Errors, and have

have fo bewildered the Minds of the People, that they will fcarce liften to any Thing in Favour of our Church. He fays, He has exerted his beft Endeavours to refute their Errors, and written a fmall Tract, collected from the beft Authors he could find there, in Defence of the Baptifm of our Church ; 400 Copies of which he difperfed *gratis* through the Province, for Want of Dr. *Wall's Abridgment*. This, for fome Time, he fays, checked their Proceedings ; but fuch a Spirit of rafh Judging and Cenforioufnefs ; fuch a Notion of Infpiration, Vifions, and of their Sect being the Elect of God, is gone out amongft them, that nothing but Time will convince them to, the contrary. Mr. *Stewart* obferves, That Books, in Defence of the Articles and Rubric of our Church, can be no where better beftowed than in that Province : Several of which Kind have been fent him by the Society.

South Carolina.

The Rev. Mr. *Garden*, the Society's Miffionary at St. *Thomas's*, in his Letter dated *April* 3, 1761, hopes the Society will excufe his Neglect of Writing, wholly owing to a tedious Indifpofition with which it pleafed God to afflict him, and which induced him, with the Advice of his Parifhioners and Phyficians, to make Ufe of the Society's Indulgence to him, and go Northward in Hopes a Change of Air might be a Means, under God, of removiug his Diforder. In this Tour he and Mr. *Durand*, who accompanied
him,

him, visited as many of the Clergy of the Church of *England*, as fell in their Way, and officiated in as many vacant Churches as their Strength would allow. Mr. *Robert Smith* of *Charles Town*, and Mr. *Warren* of St. *James Santé*, were so good as to supply Mr. *Garden*'s Church in his Absence, who, though he reaped but little immediate Benefit from his Journey, did not despair of getting over his troublesome Disorder. The Rev. Mr. *Durand*, the Society's Missionary at St. *John's*, likewise acquaints the Society, in his Letter dated *Jan.* 1, 1761, That he had made a Visit Northward for the Recovery of his Health, accompanied by Mr. *Garden*. Mr. *Durand* reports, That they had the Pleasure to find the Church flourishing in the several Places they visited, and to learn, that the Missionaries behaved well in their Stations. His People received him gladly on his Return to them, and it gave him much Pleasure to see in the Church-yard, Materials lying ready for building a new Church.

The Rev. Mr. *Harrison*, the Society's Missionary at St. *James's Goose Creek*, in his Letter of *Jan.* 26, 1761, writes, That by the Calamities of the War with the *Cherokee Indians*, the Number of Inhabitants in his Parish is considerably lessened, many of the unfortunate People, who were driven from their Settlements, having retired to the Northern Provinces, to procure that Protection and Maintenance, which they saw but little Likelihood of in *South Carolina*. He has 31 White, and 26 Black Communicants;

has

has baptized fince his laft 15 Children, and 2 Adult Negroes.

The Rev. Mr. *Baron*, the Society's Miffionary at St. *Bartholomew's*, in his Letter dated *Jan.* 12, 1761, acknowledges, That he had not been fo exact in his Correfpondence with the Society, as their Directions require, and promifes to obferve them for the Future. He writes, That he had baptized 50 in the preceding Year, and that his Communicants are about 70, of whom 50 actually communicated on *Chriftmas-Day*. He adds, That he had been bleffed in general with good Health, and faithfully endeavoured to anfwer the good Defigns of the Society in fending him thither, and has the Pleafure to affure them, that through God's Bleffing his Labours have not been in vain.

The Rev. Mr. *Martyn*, late the Society's Miffionary at St. *Andrew's*, his Affairs calling him to *England*, attended the General Meeting of the Society in *September* 1761, refigned the Miffionary's Salary, thinking the Minifter of St. *Andrew* fufficiently provided for without the Society's Allowance; and received their Thanks for his paft good Conduct, as well as his generous Behaviour on this Occafion.

Georgia.

By a Letter from the Rev. Mr. *Zouberbubler*, late the Society's Miffionary at *Savannah*, dated *June* 24, 1761, it appears, That the Rev. Mr. *Duncanfon*, whom the Society had appointed for
that

that Miffion, was not then arrived there; and
Mr. *Zouberbuhler*, that his Parifhioners might
not be left without a Minifter, had fubmitted to
defer his coming to *England* to another Year.
And by Letters from Mr. *Duncanfon* himfelf,
which he wrote in *April* and *May* laft, it is plain
he had not then received Notice of his Appoint-
ment to *Georgia*. But by a Letter from the
Rev. Mr. *Carter*, *Aug.* 18, 1761, we learn, That
Mr. *Duncanfon* fet Sail from the *Bahama's* to
Georgia at that Time, where, we hear, he is
fince arrived : But what Reception he has met
with from the Governor of *Georgia*, the Society
have not yet had certain Intelligence.

Bahama Iflands.

The Society have received a Letter from his
Excellency Mr. *Shirley*, Governor of the *Bahamas*,
dated *New Providence*, *Jan.* 15, 1761, in which
he writes, That the whole *Bahama* Iflands form
but one Parifh, which confifts of *New Providence*, *Eleuthera* diftant from it 30 Leagues, and
Harbour Ifland diftant from it 25 Leagues, and
the two laft diftant from each other about 20
Leagues, and the Navigation between them all
dangerous. In *New Providence* are 300 Families, having one Church in the Town of *Naffau*,
at eight Miles Diftance from the Eaftern Inhabitants of the Ifland, who can feldom attend
Divine Service there. Therefore the Miffionary
officiates to them once a Month at a private
Houfe. But the other Duties of the Miniftry
occur

occur fo frequently in *New Providence*, that no one Man can difcharge them in fo regular a Manner as is to be wifhed. *Eleuthera* contains 70 Families, fo difperfed along the Coaft, that they cannot all be vifited without great Difficulty. *Harbour Ifland* contains near 60 Families, who refide all upon one Spot. While the Miffionary makes a Vifit to each of the two laft Iflands of 18 or 20 Days twice in the Year, as well as the Time taken up in his Voyages thither and back again, the Cure of *New Providence* is unfupplied, and the People thereby contract an Indifference to Religion by his Abfence, the ill Effect of which in *NewProvidence*, it is to be feared, is much greater than the good Effect arifing from his fhort Refidence in the other Iflands, which muft be reckoned among the dark Corners of the Earth, fo long as there fhall be but one Minifter refident in the *Bahama* Iflands, even fuppofing him to be never abfent, and always in good Health. This the Governor thought it incumbent on him to reprefent to the Society; and to recommend the State of Religion in his Government, as an Object worthy of their Regard. He thinks a Catechift (who might likewife do the Duty of a Schoolmafter) if fixed at *Harbour Ifland*, might be fufficient for their Inftruction, provided a Miffionary refided at *Eleuthera*, who might occafionally vifit *Harbour Ifland*, being convinced that the Miffionary, who has the Cure of *New Providence*, cannot confiftently vifit either of thofe Iflands. Concern-

I   ing

ing Mr. *Carter* the Governor writes, That the
News of his being directed to leave *New Pro-*
vidence gave him ſo great Concern, that he could
not avoid expoſtulating with him, and letting
him know he could not conſent to his leaving
the Colony, at leaſt not before the actual Arrival of a new Miſſionary. He excuſes himſelf
to the Society for interpoſing ſo far ; as he finds
Mr. *Carter* endowed with all the neceſſary Ta-
lents for performing the Duty of the Cure of
that Iſland with Succeſs. He takes the further
Liberty of requeſting the Society, that he may
be continued a Miſſionary among them, what-
ever they may determine concerning another
Miſſionary at *Eleuthera,* and a Catechiſt at
Harbour Iſland.

The Society, willing to do every Thing in
their Power to promote the pious Deſigns for
which they are incorporated, will take this Af-
fair into Conſideration, when they are informed
what Engagements the Inhabitants of *Eleuthera*
and *Harbour Iſland* will. enter into towards the
Support of a Miniſter and Schoolmaſter among
them, agreeable to the conſtant Rules of the
Society.

☞   The Society, from their firſt Inſtitution, taking into their ſerious Conſideration the abſolute
Neceſſity there is, that thoſe Clergymen, who
ſhall be ſent abroad, ſhall be duly qualified for
the Work to which they are appointed, deſires
every one, who recommends any Perſon to them
for

for that Purpofe, to teftify their Knowledge, as to the following Particulars :

1. The Age of the Perfon.
2. His Condition of Life, whether fingle or married.
3. His Temper.
4. His Prudence.
5. His Learning.
6. His fober and pious Converfation.
7. His Zeal for the Chriftian Religion, and Diligence in his holy Calling.
8. His Affection to the prefent Government.
9. His Conformity to the Doctrine and Difcipline of the, Church of *England.*

And the Society doth now requeft, and earneftly befeech all Perfons concerned, that they recommend no Man out of Favour or Affection, or any other worldly Confideration, but with a fince Regard to the Honour of Almighty G o d and our bleffed S a v i o u r ; as they tender the Intereft of the Chriftian Religion, and the Good of Men's Souls.

And the Society particularly defire their Friends in *America* to be fo juft to them, when any Perfon appears there in the Character of a Clergyman of the Church of *England,* but by his Behaviour difgraces that Character, to examine as far as may be into his Letters of Orders, his Name and Circumftances, and to infpect the

I 2   publick

publick Liſt of the Names of the Miſſionaries of
this ˙Society, publiſhed annually with the Abſtract of their Proceedings ; and the Society are
fully pérſuaded it will appear, that ſuch unwor-
thy Perſon came thither without their Knowledge ; but if it ſhould happen, that any ſuch
ſhould come thither from them, they intreat
their Friends in *America*, in the ſacred Name of
Chriſt, to inform them, and they will *put away
from them that wicked Perſon.*

The Receipts and Payments on the General Account of the Society for the Year paſt, ſtood
thus at the Audit of the Society on the 28th
Day of *January* 1762.

R E C E I P T S.

	l.	*s.*	*d.*
By Ballance in the Hands of the Treaſurer on the 28th Day of *January*, 1761, ——— —	189	10	7
By Benefactions and Legacies in the Year 1761, ——— —	1680	10	6
By Subſcriptions of Members of the Society, ——— —	645	4	0
By Rent from Tenants, and by Dividends in the publick Funds,	805	18	4
By Sale of 3000 *l.* Old *South-Sea* Annuities at 76*l.* 10*s. per Cent.*	2295	0	0
Total	5616	3	5

PAYMENTS.

	l.	s.	d.
By Salaries to Miffionaries, Cate-chifts, Schoolmafters, and the Officers of the Society, ———	4249	0	6
By Books, Gratuities to Miffiona-ries, and other accidental Charges,	433	19	2
By the Maintenance and Education of two Negro Youths under the Care of the Rev. Mr. *Moore*,—	71	8	7
By two Legacies in *Eaft-India* and Old *South Sea* Annuities given in this Year ftill remaining there,	200	0	0
	4954	8	3
By Ballance in the Hands of the Treafurer on the General Account of the Society on the 28th Day of *January*, 1762, ——	661	15	2
Total	5616	3	5

Abſtract of the Society's *London* Account relating to *Codrington* College and their Plantations in *Barbadoes*, as ballanced by the Audi-
tors of the Society, on the 28th Day of
January, 1762.

The Society to the Truſt   Dr.

	l.	*s.*	*d.*
To Ballance of Accounts on the 28th Day of *January*, 1761,	2994	19	6¼
To Old *South-Sea* Annuities, in-cluding 3000 *l.* purchaſed *Feb.* 23, 1761, ——	6000	0	0
To net Produce of 131 Caſks of Clayed Sugars ſold at *London*, —— ——	2976	5	3
To Dividends on the ſaid 6000*l.* Annuities for one Year, due *October* 10, 1761, ——	180	0	0
£.	12,151	4	9¼

The Society to the Truſt Cr.

	l.	*s.*	*d.*
By Purchaſe of 3000 *l.* Old *South-Sea* Annuities at 76 *l.* 10 *s. per Cent. Feb.* 23, 1761,	2295	o	o
By Salaries to Profeſſors at *Codrington* College, —— ——	135	o	o
By Ditto to Officers in *London*,——	75	o	o
By Invoice of Goods ſent to *Barbadoes*, —— ——	235	7	8
By Commiſſion at 2¼ *per Cent.*——	5	17	8
By petty Diſburſements, ——	7	9	2
By 6000 *l.* Old *South-Sea* Annuities remaining in the Name of the Society, ——	6000	o	o
By Caſh in the Hands of the Society's Treaſurer, *January* 28, 1762, —— ——	3397	10	3¼

£ 12,151   4   9¼

Barbadoes.

Barbadoes.

The Society have suffered a great Loss by the Death of Mr. *Hodgson*, a Gentleman, who had filled his Station, as Usher to the School and Catechist to the Negroes in the Society's Plantations, with Ability and Integrity. His Place is supplied by Mr. *Davis*, a Scholar upon the Foundation of *Codrington* College, who is very useful (above his Age) in instructing the Boys ; to whom the Society have agreed to give a handsome Gratuity for his Trouble, till Notice shall arrive, that the Rev. Mr. *Duke*, who is now resident upon the Island, is chosen to succeed Mr. *Hodgson*. The Attorneys have appointed a Master to teach Writing and Arithmetic in the College, which the Society have approved of, and have given the fullest Orders for a Supply of every Thing that is wanting, according to the Judgment of the Attorneys, and hope in Time to bring their Plantations to such Perfection, as may enable them to fulfil their Trust in the amplest Manner.

A LIST

A LIST of the

MEMBERS

OF

The SOCIETY *for the Propagation of the Gospel in Foreign Parts.*

Those marked thus * were chosen Members in the Year 1761.

A.

THE Right Reverend *Richard* Lord Bishop of St. *Asaph.*
Fifield Allen, D. D. Archdeacon of *Middlesex.*
Thomas Archer, M. A. Prebendary of *St. Paul's.*
Francis Astry, D. D. Treasurer of St. *Paul's.*
Francis Ayscough, D. D. Dean of *Bristol.*
William Ayerst, D. D. Prebendary of *Canterbury.*
Charles Ward Apthorp, of *New York,* Esq;
John Apthorp, of *London,* Esq;
James Apthorp, of *Boston,* Esq;
East Apthorp, M. A. Fellow of *Jesus College* in
K   *Cambridge*

Cambridge in *England,* and Miſſionary to the Church of *Cambridge* in *New England.*
James Auſc, of *Great Torrington* in *Devonſhire,* Eſq;.

B.

THE Right Honourable *William* Earl of *Bath.*

The Right Reverend *Edward* Lord Biſhop of *Bath* and *Wells.*

The Right Reverend *John* Lord Biſhop of *Bangor.*

The Right Reverend *Thomas* Lord Biſhop of *Briſtol.*

Sir *John Barnard* Knt. Alderman of *London.*

The Honourable *Francis Barnard* Eſq; Governor of the Province of *Maſſachuſet's Bay* in *New England.*

* The Honourable and Reverend *Shute Barrington,* Canon of *Chriſt Church.*

* *Richard Barford,* D. D.

Edward Ballard, D. D.

Thomas Barnard, M. A. Rector of the Church of *Bridge Town* in *Barbadoes.*

Mr. *James Barclay,* M. A.

Mr. *Solomon Barton,* Merchant.

Cutts Barton, D. D.

John Bradſtreet, Eſq; Colonel.

Joſeph Forſter Barham, Eſq;

* *Edward Bearcroft,* Eſq;

Philip Bearcroft, M. A.

George Berkeley, M. A.

John

John Berriman, M. A.
John Berney, D. D. Archdeacon of *Norwich*.
Calverley Bewicke, Efq;
Thomas Birch, D. D. F. R. S.
Thomas Blackwell, M. A.
Ebenezer Blackwell, Efq;
Jonathan Blenman, Efq; Attorney-General in *Barbadoes.*
Robert Bolton, LL. D. Dean of *Carlifle.*
Penifton Booth, D. D. Dean of *Windfor.*
William Bowles, M. A. Fellow of *Winchefter* College.
William Brakenridge, D. D.
Robert Breton, M. A. Archdeacon of *Hereford.*
Henry Burrough, M. A. Prebendary of *Peterborough.*
Jofeph Browne, D. D. Provoft of *Queen's* College in *Oxford.*
John Burton, D. D. Fellow of *Eaton College.*
Thomas Burton, D.D. Archdeacon of St. *David's.*

C.

THE moft Reverend *Thomas* Lord Archbifhop of *Canterbury.*
The moft Reverend *Michael* Lord Archbifhop of *Cafhel.*
The Right Reverend *Charles* Lord Bifhop of *Carlifle.*
The Right Reverend *Edmund* Lord Bifhop of *Chefter.*
The Right Reverend *William* Lord Bifhop of *Chichefter.*

The

The Right Honourable Lord *Colrayne.*
The Honourable *George Clinton,* Efq; Admiral.
John Chapman, D. D. Archdeacon of *Sudbury.*
Angel Chauncey, D. D. Prebendary of *Salifbury.*
Timothy Collins, M. A. Canon Refidentiary of
    Wells.
Mr. *John Cobb.*
Edward Cobden, D. D. Archdeacon of *London.*
Edward Codrington, Efq;
John Cookfey, M. A.
Charles Walter Congreve, M. A. Archdeacon of
    Armagh.
Allen Cowper, M. A.
John Craven, M. A.
Samuel Crefwick, D. D. Dean of *Wells.*
Lewis Crufius, D. D. Prebendary of *Worcefter.*

D.

THE moft Reverend *Charles* Lord Arch-
    bifhop of *Dublin.*
The Right Honourable *William* Earl of *Dart-
    mouth.*
The Right Reverend and Honourable *Richard*
    Lord Bifhop of *Durham.*
The Right Reverend *Samuel* Lord Bifhop of
    St, *David's.*
The Honourable *Wriothefley Digby,* Efq; LL. D.
The Honourable *Arthur Dobbs,* Efq; Governor
    of *North Carolina.*
John Dalton, D. D. Prebendary of *Worcefter.*
Richard Dalton, Efq;
                                   Chriftopher

Chriſtopher Dawſon, Eſq;
Peter d'Eſpaignol, Eſq;
John Denne, D. D. Archdeacon of *Rocheſter.*
Samuel Dickens, D. D. Archdeacon of *Durham.*
George Dixon, D. D. Principal of *Edmund Hall,*
 in *Oxford.*
Thomas D'oyly, D. D. Archdeacon of *Lewis.*
Thomas Drake, D. D.
Philip Duval, LL. B.
Robert Dinwiddie, Eſq;

E.

THE, Right Reverend *Mathias* Lord Biſhop
 of *Ely.*
The Right Reverend *George* Lord Biſhop of
 Exeter.
John Emerſon, M. A.
Jucks Egerton, M. A.
Sloane Elſemere, D. D.
George Errington, Eſq;

F.

* THE Right Honourable the Lord Viſcount
 Folkſtone.
Frederick Frankland, Eſq;.
John Fountayne, D. D. Dean of *York.*
William Freind, D. D. Dean of *Canterbury.*
Tobias Frere, Eſq;.
Thomas Edwards Freeman, Eſq;.
The Rev. Mr. *Folds.*

THE

G.

THE Right Honourable *John* Earl *Granville.*

The Right Reverend *William* Lord Biſhop of *Gloceſter.*

Henry Galley, D. D. Prebendary of *Gloceſter.*

William Geekee, D. D. Archdeacon of *Gloceſter.*

Edmund Gibſon, M. A. Precentor of St. *Paul's.*

John Griffith, D. D. Prebendary of *Canterbury.*

Mr. *Benjamin Goodiſon.*

John Gooch, M. A. Prebendary of *Ely.*

Sir *Francis Goſling,* Knt. Alderman of *London.*

David Gregory, D. D. Dean of *Chriſt Church, Oxon.*

Thomas Greene, D. D. Dean of *Saliſbury.*

Blinman Greſley, M. A.

H.

THE Right Honourable *George Montagu Dunk,* Earl of *Halifax.*

The Right Honourable and Right Reverend *James* Lord Biſhop of *Hereford.*

The Honourable and Reverend *John Harley,* M. A. Archdeacon of *Salop.*

The Honourable *James Hamilton,* Eſq; Governor of *Pennſylvania.*

Sir *Thomas Harriſon,* Knt. Chamberlain of *London.*

Hugh Hall, of *Boſton* in *New England,* Eſq;.

James

James Hallifax, D. D.
George Harrison, of the City of *New York*, Efq;
Bartholomew Hammond, Efq;
Benjamin Hayes, Efq;
Mr. *George Hayter*.
John Head, D. D. Archdeacon of *Canterbury.*
* *William Henry*, D. D.
William Herring, D. D. Dean of St. *Afaph.*
Thomas Herring, M. A.
* *Samuel Holcombe*, M.A. Prebendary of *Worcefter*.
Richard Hotchkis, M. A.
Jofeph Hudfon, Efq; Major General.
William Weftern, Hugeffen Efq;
William Hutton, M. A.

I.

SIR *Edmund Ifham*, Bart.
Stephen Theodore Janffen, Efq; Alderman of
London.
Charles Jenner, D. D. Archdeacon of *Huntingdon.*
Laurence Jackfon, B. D. Prebendary of *Lincoln.*
Samuel Johnfon, D. D. Prefident of the College for
the Education of Youth in the City of *New York.*

K.

THE Right Honourable *Thomas* Earl of
Kinnoul.
The Honourable and Reverend *Frederic Keppel*,
Canon of *Windfor*.
Anthony Keck, Efq; Serjeant at Law.

THE

L.

THE Right Reverend *Richard* Lord Bishop
of *London.*

The Right Reverend *Frederick* Lord Bishop of
Lichfield and *Coventry.*

The Right Reverend *John* Lord Bishop of
Landaff.

The Right Reverend *William* Lord Bishop of
Londonderry.

Robert Lamb, LL. D. Dean of *Peterborough.*

John Lawrey, M. A. Prebendary of *Rochester.*

William Lloyd, M. A.

M.

THE Right Honourable *Charles* Lord *May-
nard.*

Margaret Professor of Divinity, *Oxon.*

Margaret Professor of Divinity, *Cambridge.*

Alexander Macaulay, Esq;.

William Markham, D. D. Prebendary of *Durham.*

Ossory Medlicot, M. A.

John Frederick Miege, D. D. Protestant Ecclesi-
astical Counsellor to the Elector *Palatin.*

Jeremiah Milles, D. D. Presentor of *Exeter.*

John Myonnet, M. A.

Charles Moss, D. D. Archdeacon of *Colchester.*

Roger

Roger Moſtyn, M. A.
Daniel Moore, Eſq;
Thomas Moore, D. D.
John Moore, M. A.
Charles Morton, M. D. and F. R. S.
John Morgan, B. D. Chancellor of St. *David's.*
Thomas Moriſon, M. A.

N.

THE moſt Noble *Thomas Holles* Duke of *Newcaſtle.*

The Right Reverend *Philip* Lord Biſhop of *Norwich.*

Stephen Niblet, D.D. Warden of *All Souls* College in *Oxford.*

Gerard Neden, D. D.

Samuel Nicolls, LL. D. Rector of St. *James Weſtminſter.*

John Nicoll, D. D. Prebendary of *Weſtminſter.*

John Nicols, D. D. Preacher of the *Charter-Houſe.*

O.

THE Right Reverend *John* Lord Biſhop of *Oxford.*

The Honourable *James Oglethorpe,* Eſq; Lieutenant General.

L THE

P.

THE Right Reverend *Richard* Lord Bifhop
of *Peterborough.*
The Right Honourable Sir *Thomas Parker*, Lord
Chief Baron of the *Exchequer.*
Sir *John Philipps*, Bart.
Thomas Pardo, D. D. Principal of *Jefus* College,
Oxon.
Vincent Perronet, M. A.
Jonathan Perrie, Efq;
The Reverend *James Perard*, M. A. Chaplain to
the King of *Pruffia.*
Charles Plumptree, D. D. Archdeacon of *Ely.*
Edward Poole, M. A. Prebendary of *Brecknock.*
John Potter, D. D. Archdeacon of *Oxford.*
John Pownall, Efq; Secretary to the Lords of
Trade and Plantations.
The Hon. *Thomas Pownall*, Efq; Governor of
South Carolina.

R.

THE Right Reverend *Zachary* Lord Bifhop
of *Rochefter*, and Dean of *Weftminfter.*
Sir *Thomas Robinfon*, Bart.
Thomas Rawlinfon, Efq; Alderman of *London.*
Thomas Randolph, D.D. Prefident of *Corpus Chrifti*
College in *Oxford.*
Regius Profeffor of Divinity, *Oxon.*
Regius Profeffor of Divinity, *Cambridge.*

John

John Richards, D. D.
William Richardson, D. D. Mafter of *Emanuel*
   College, *Cambridge.*
Nicolas Robinson, M. D.
William Robinson, Efq;.
Mr. *John Rofs* of *Philadelphia.*
John Rutherford, M. A.

S.

THE Right Reverend *John* Lord Bifhop of
   Salifbury.
The Honourable *William Shirley,* Efq; Governor
   of the *Bahama Iflands.*
Samuel Salter, D. D. Mafter of the *Charter-*
   houfe.
Erafmus Sanders, D. D. Prebendary of *Rochefter.*
* *George Secker,* M. A. Prebendary of *Canter-*
   bury.
William Simpfon, D. D.
Jonathan Shipley, LL. D. Dean of *Winchefter.*
William Smith, D. D. Provoft of the College for
   the Education of Youth in the City of *Phila-*
   delphia.
Henry Stebbing, D. D. Chancellor of *Salifbury.*
Samuel Stedman, D. D. Prebendary of *Canterbury.*
Mathew Stewart of *N. London,* Merchant.
Adlard Squire Stukeley, Efq;
Jofeph Sims, M. A. Prebendary of St. *Paul's.*
John Simpfon, M. A.

T.

S I R *John Thorold*, Bart.
Thomas *Tanner*, D. D. Prebendary of *Can-terbury.*
Mr. St. *George Talbot*, of *New York.*
John Tatterfall, M. A.
John Taylor, LL. D. Chancellor of *Lincoln.*
Edmund Tew, D. D.
John Thomlinfon, M. A.
John Thomlinfon, Efq;
John Thomlinfon, jun. Efq;
James Torkington, M. A.
Hugh Thomas, D. D. Dean of *Ely.*
John Thomas, D. D. Prebendary of *Weftminfter.*
John Thornton, Efq;
John Torriano, Efq;
Chauncey Townfhend, Efq;
Thomas Tounfon, B. D.
James Tunftal, D. D. Treafurer of St. *David's,*
Barlow Trecothick, Efq;
Jofiah Tucker, D. D. Dean of *Glocefter.*

V.

P*Hilip de Valois*, M. A.
Henry Vane, D. D. Prebendary of *Durham.*
Abbot Upfher, M. A.

THE

W.

THE Right Reverend *James* Lord Biſhop of *Worceſter.*

The Right Reverend *Richard* Lord Biſhop of *Waterford.*

The Honourable *Benning Wentworth*, Eſq; Governor of *New Hampſhire* in *New England.*

Francis Walwyn, D. D. Prebendary of *Canterbury.*

Henry Waterland, LL. B. Prebendary of *Briſtol.*

John Waugh, D. D. Dean of *Worceſter.*

John Wilberfoſs, Eſq;

Chriſtopher Wilſon, D. D. Canon Reſidentiary of St. *Paul*'s.

Thomas Williams, of *Merthyr*, Prebendary of *Brecknock.*

John Wills, M. A.

Mr. *John Willis.*

Edward Wilſon, M. A.

Thomas Wilſon, D. D. Prebendary of *Weſtminſter.*

Granville Wheeler, M. A.

Samuel Wolley, M. A. Prebendary of *Worceſter.*

Y.

THE moſt Reverend *Robert* Lord Archbiſhop of *York.*

Francis Yarborough, D. D. Principal of *Brazen-Noſe* College, *Oxford.*

Edward

Edward Yardley, B. D. Archdeacon of *Cardigan*.
Edward Younge, LL. D. Clerk of the Clofet to
the Princefs Dowager of *Wales*.

Ladies Annual Subfcribers,

L ADY *Curzon*.
The Honourable Mrs. *Shirley*.
Mrs. *Cotton* of *Etwall* in *Derbyſhire*,
Mrs. *Apthorp* of *Hatton Garden*.
Miſs *Cordelia Bright*.
Mrs. *Gordon*.

A LIST of the

BISHOPS, DEANS, &c.

Who have PREACHED before

The SOCIETY *for the Propagation of the Gospel in Foreign Parts.*

Anno

1701 THE Reverend Dr. *Willis*, Dean of *Lincoln*.

1702 The Lord Bishop of *Worcester*, Dr. *Lloyd*, not printed.

1703 The Lord Bishop of *Sarum*, Dr. *Burnet*.

1704 The Lord Bishop of *Lichfield* and *Coventry*, Dr. *Hough*.

1705 The Lord Bishop of *Chichester*, Dr. *Williams*.

1706 The Lord Bishop of St *Asaph*, Dr. *Beveridge*.

1707 The Reverend Dr. *Stanley*, Dean of St. *Asaph*.

1708 The Lord Bishop of *Chester*, Sir *William Dawes*.

1709 The Lord Bishop of *Norwich*, Dr. *Trimnel*.

1710 The Lord Bishop of St *Asaph*, Dr *Fleetwood*.

1711

1711 The Reverend Dr. *Kennet*, Dean of *Pe-terborough.*

1712 The Lord Biſhop of *Ely*, Dr. *Moore.*

1713 The Reverend Dr. *Stanhope*, Dean of *Canterbury.*

1714 The Lord Biſhop of *Clogher*, Dr. *Aſh.*

1715 The Reverend Dr. *Sherlock*, Dean of *Chicheſter.*

1716 The Reverend Mr. *Hayley*, Canon Reſidentiary of *Chicheſter.*

1717 The Lord Biſhop of *Hereford*, Dr. *Biſſe.*

1718 The Lord Biſhop of *Lichfield* and *Coventry*, Dr. *Chandler.*

1719 The Lord Biſhop of *Carliſle*, Dr. *Bradford.*

1720 The Reverend Dr. *Waddington.*

1721 The Lord Biſhop of *Briſtol*, Dr. *Bolter.*

1722 The Reverend Dr. *Waugh*, Dean of *Gloceſter.*

1723 The Lord Biſhop of *Ely*, Dr. *Greene.*

1724 The Lord Biſhop of St. *Aſaph*, Dr. *Wynn.*

1725 The Lord Biſhop of *Gloceſter*, Dr. *Wilcocks.*

1726 The Lord Biſhop of *Norwich*, Dr. *Leng.*

1727 The Lord Biſhop of *Lincoln*, Dr. *Reynolds.*

1728 The Lord Biſhop of *Hereford*, Dr. *Egerton.*

1729 The Reverend Dr. *Pearce.*

1730 The Reverend Dr. *Denne*, Archdeacon of *Rocheſter.*

1731

1731 The Reverend Dr. *Berkeley*, Dean of *Londonderry*.
1732 The Lord Bishop of *Lichfield* and *Coventry*, Dr. *Smallbrooke*.
1733 The Reverend Dr. *Maddox*, Dean of *Wells*.
1734 The Lord Bishop of *Chichester*, Dr. *Hare*.
1735 The Reverend Dr. *Lynch*, Dean of *Canterbury*.
1736 The Lord Bishop of St.*David's*, Dr.*Claggett*
1737 The Lord Bishop of *Bangor*, Dr. *Herring*.
1738 The Lord Bishop of *Bristol*, Dr. *Butler*.
1739 The Lord Bishop of *Glocester*, Dr. *Benson*.
1740 The Lord Bishop of *Oxford*, Dr. *Secker*.
1741 The Reverend Dr. *Stebbing*, Chancellor of *Sarum*.
1742 The Lord Bishop of *Chichester*, Dr.*Mawson*.
1743 The Lord Bishop of *Landaff*, Dr. *Gilbert*
1744 The Reverend Dr. *Bearcroft*, Secretary of the Society.
1745 The Lord Bishop of *Bangor*, Dr.*Hutton*.
1746 The Lord Bishop of *Lincoln*, Dr.*Thomas*.
1747 The Lord Bishop of St. *Asaph*, Dr. *Lisle*.
1748 The Reverend Dr.*George*, Dean of *Lincoln*.
1749 The Lord Bishop of St.*David's*, Dr.*Trevor*.
1750 The Lord Bishop of *Peterborough*, Dr. *Thomas*.
1752 The Lord Bishop of *Carlisle*, Dr.*Osbaldiston*.

M   1753

1753   The Lord Bifhop of *Landaff,* Dr. *Creffet.*

1754   The Lord Bifhop of St. *Afaph,* Dr. *Drummond.*

1755   The Lord Bifhop of *Norwich,* Dr. *Hayter.*

1756   The Lord Bifhop of *Lichfield* and *Coventry,* Dr. *Cornwallis.*

1757   The Lord Bifhop of *Chefter,* Dr. *Keene.*

1758   The Lord Bifhop of *Glocefter,* Dr. *Johnfon.*

1759   The Lord Bifhop of St. *David's,* Dr. *Ellis.*

1760   The Lord Bifhop of *Chichefter,* Dr. *Afhburnham.*

1761   The Lord Bifhop of *Landaff,* Dr. *Newcome.*

1762   The Lord Bifhop of *Oxford,* Dr. *Hume.*

The Form of a LEGACY to this SOCIETY.

ITEM, *I give to* the Incorporated SOCIETY, for the Propagation of the Gospel in Foreign Parts, *the Sum of*   to *be raised and paid by and out of all my ready Money, Plate, Goods, and Personal Effects, which by Law I may or can charge with the Payment of the same* (and not out of any Part of my Lands, Tenements, or Hereditaments) *and to be applied towards carrying on the Charitable Purposes for which the said Society was Incorporated.*

> *N. B.* The Variation in this Form of a LEGACY, from that formerly printed, is made necessary, on Account of some late unhappy Mistakes in Wills, by which several considerable Legacies have been lost to the Society, and the good Intentions of the Testators have been intirely defeated, because the Sums bequeathed to the Society have been ordered to be raised, or paid out of Lands, or Real Estates, which is not now permitted by Law.

Direct to *Edward Pearson*, Esq; in *Duke Street*, *Westminster*, their TREASURER.

And to the Reverend Dr. *Daniel Burton* in *Bartlet's Buildings*, *Holborn*, their SECRETARY.